FLASH MX

in easy steps

NICK VANDOME

In easy steps is an imprint of Computer Step
Southfield Road . Southam
Warwickshire CV47 0FB . England

http://www.ineasysteps.com

Notice of Liability
Every effort has been made to ensure that this book contains accurate and current information. However, Computer Step and the author shall not be liable for any loss or damage suffered by readers as a result of any information contained herein.

Trademarks
Flash™ is a trademark of Macromedia Inc. All other trademarks are acknowledged as belonging to their respective companies.

Printed and bound in the United Kingdom

ISBN 1-84078-229-3

Contents

Introducing Flash   7

1

The evolution of Flash   8
How Flash works   9
The uses for Flash   10
What Flash can do   11
Obtaining Flash   12
Installing Flash   13
The Flash environment   14

Getting started   15

2

The Timeline   16
The Stage   17
Tools and toolbars   20
The Menu bar   21
Properties Inspector   22
Panels   23
Viewing options   24
QuickStart templates   25
Accessibility   27

Creating objects   29

3

Stage and overlay objects   30
Tools panel   34
Line tool   35
Pen tool   36
Subselect tool   37
Oval tool   38
Rectangle tool   39
Pencil tool   40
Brush tool   42
Ink Bottle tool   43
Paint Bucket tool   44
Dropper tool   45
Eraser tool   46

Editing objects 47

4

Selecting with the Arrow tool 48
Selecting with the Lasso tool 50
Grouping objects 51
Free Transform tool 52
Reshaping objects 54
Aligning objects 56
Pixel snapping 57
Stacking order 58
Cut-aways 59
Paste in Place 60

Colour and text 61

5

Standard Color palette 62
Adding solid colours 63
Adding gradients 65
Fill Transform tool 67
More colour options 69
Selecting colours 70
Adding text 71
Formatting text 73
Manipulating text 74

Symbols and instances 75

6

Symbols and instances defined 76
The Library 78
Converting objects to symbols 82
Creating a new symbol 84
Symbol Editing Mode 86
Editing symbols 87
Editing instances 88

Bitmaps, sound and video 89

7

Using bitmaps 90
Importing bitmaps 91
Bitmap properties 92
Bitmaps as fills 93
Using sound 95

Importing sounds	96
Editing sounds	97
Adding video	99
Manipulating video	100

Frames and layers — 101

8

Working with frames	102
Adding frames	105
Deleting and copying frames	107
Frame properties	108
About layers	109
Working with layers	110
Inserting layers	111
Deleting and copying layers	112
Layer modes	113
Layer properties	114
Layers folders	115
Mask layers	116

Animation — 119

9

Animation basics	120
Elements of animation	121
Scenes	124
Frame-by-frame animation	126
Motion tweening	129
Motion guides	132
Motion guide orientation	134
Shape tweening	135
Animating text	138
Distribute text to layers	139
Movie clips	141

Interactivity — 143

10

Types of interactivity	144
Frame actions	145
Adding Stop and Play actions	148
Adding Go To actions	149
Inserting a preloader	151

Button symbols   153
Adding actions to buttons   156
Adding movie clips and sounds   158
Creating disjoint rollovers   159
Adding invisible buttons   160
Creating rollover navigation bars   161
ActionScript   164
UI Components   166
Named anchors   168
Movie Explorer   170

Testing and publishing   171

Testing options   172
Testing environment   174
Preparing to publish   178
More publishing options   182
Creating a transparent movie   183
Publishing a movie   185
Publishing on the Web   186

Index   187

11

Introducing Flash

This chapter gives an overview of the functions of Flash MX and the uses to which it can be put. It shows how to obtain and install the program and gives details of the Flash environment when it is first opened.

Covers

The evolution of Flash | 8

How Flash works | 9

The uses for Flash | 10

What Flash can do | 11

Obtaining Flash | 12

Installing Flash | 13

The Flash environment | 14

Chapter One

The evolution of Flash

If there is one constant about the Internet and the World Wide Web it is the speed at which they develop. As recently as the beginning of the 1990s Web users were excited about the possibility of viewing coloured static text and a few small, equally static, images. However, since then website designers and developers have harnessed advances in technology with a desire to create increasingly complicated multimedia output. This includes animated images, animated text, page transitions, sound and video.

Initially, even the most basic multimedia effects on the Web came at a price: downloading time. In a lot of cases the infrastructure for downloading multimedia pages was just not up to the task, with the result that these types of pages took a long time to appear on the user's computer. The result of this was a lot of annoyed users and a lot of sites that were left unvisited because they took too long to download.

Bandwidth is a term used to describe the amount of digital data that can be sent down a telephone cable and the speed at which it is sent. A higher bandwidth means that more information can be sent down a cable, and so reach the user's computer more quickly.

Since multimedia files can be a lot larger than their static counterparts, increased bandwidth is vital for them to download quickly enough to keep the user's attention.

But as with everything on the Web, the technology has not been slow to catch up and, due to increased bandwidth for downloading and more advanced browsers for viewing, it is now possible to enjoy truly exceptional multimedia experiences on the Web, without having to wait an eternity for the files to download.

In addition to increased bandwidth, software programs for creating multimedia sites have become increasingly powerful and this is where Flash comes in. Flash is an animation program that can produce high quality multimedia files. In addition to this it uses a number of techniques to ensure that the final product is as streamlined as possible, thus creating files that can be downloaded reasonably quickly. Three of the most important aspects of Flash in this respect are:

- Vector-based graphics

- Streaming

- Compression

With the release of Flash MX the program has been given even more power and versatility so that it is very firmly a design and website authoring tool.

How Flash works

Vector-based graphics

Traditionally, images on the Web have been bitmaps i.e. images that are made up of pixels, or tiny coloured dots. Since each pixel adds to the file size of the image you have to walk a fine line between quality and file size. Also, when a bitmap image is resized it can deteriorate in quality.

The three types of bitmap images that are used on the Web are GIFs (Graphical Interchange Format), JPEGs (Joint Photographic Experts Group) and PNGs (Portable Network Group).

Since one of the main functions of Flash is creating drawing objects, it is vital that it can do this in an efficient and high-quality way. It achieves this by using a vector-based system for producing graphics, rather than a pixel-based one. A vector-based system is one where objects, lines and fills are created using mathematical equations. This has two considerable advantages:

- Vector-based images are usually a lot smaller in file size than their bitmap counterparts

- Vector-based images lose very little image quality when they are resized

Streaming

The end product created by Flash (called a Flash movie) can be either a few seconds long or several minutes. With the latter there could be problems with downloading time over the Web. Flash overcomes this problem with a technique called streaming. This feeds information to the browser as it needs it to play the movie, without having to wait for the whole thing to be downloaded to get started.

A Flash file is known as a movie.

Compression

Most images on the Web are compressed in one way or another. GIFs, JPEGs and PNGs all use various forms of compression to decrease their file size. In the majority of cases this has, at worst, only a minimal effect on the final image.

Drawing programs (such as Macromedia Freehand and Adobe Illustrator) use vector-based systems for creating graphics.

Flash uses a variety of sophisticated compression techniques, for both images and sounds. The technical side of this is best left to the experts but there are some preference settings that can be used to determine various compression settings. These will be looked at in the relevant chapters.

The uses for Flash

Web authoring

Although Flash movies can be output through a variety of devices, their main function is in the production of Web pages. However, there is one important point that should be remembered in relation to this: Flash movies have to be incorporated into HTML documents to enable them to be displayed on the Web. This means you have to create the HTML pages for your site and then insert the relevant Flash movies. Luckily, Flash has a facility for producing HTML files that incorporate Flash movies and this is looked at in Chapter Eleven. The end result looks complicated, but Flash takes care of most of this behind the scenes.

Presentations

In addition to be being used on Web pages, Flash movies can also be used as a presentation tool. To do this, the Flash movie is played through a computer as a stand-alone application. This is known as creating a projector and this is a self-contained executable program that can play a movie regardless of whether the user has the Flash Player installed or not.

E-commerce

Flash contains a powerful programming language, called ActionScript, which is ideal for using on e-commerce sites that need a bit more than animations and simple interactive actions. In Flash MX, ActionScript has been enhanced so that the programming syntax is the same as for JavaScript. Therefore anyone with a knowledge of JavaScript will quickly feel at home with ActionScript. This can then be used to create complex online order forms and other elements that are integral to an e-commerce site. However, a good knowledge of programming is still needed to use this feature to its full potential.

Flash MX has been developed with a view to creating whole websites in Flash, as well as individual elements within HTML pages.

Flash movies can also be exported into video formats such as QuickTime or as a Windows .AVI movie.

What Flash can do

Animation

It is perfectly possible to produce Flash movies that contain nothing more than static text and images. However, if this is your aim you would be well advised to use a HTML program such as Dreamweaver or FrontPage if you are creating Web pages and PowerPoint if you are creating presentations. One of Flash's main reasons for existing is its ability to animate both text and graphics.

Flash offers a considerable range of techniques for animation:

- Text that fades in and out or moves across the screen

- Frame-by-frame animation, using either objects you have drawn yourself or items you import into Flash

- Tweened animation, a technique where you set the start and end point for an object and Flash automatically creates an animation between the two points. Tweened animations can be in the form of either motion or shape tweens

- Guided animation, where you create a path which the animated object can follow

A shape tween animation, also known as morphing, changes one simple shape into another during the animation.

Interactivity

Another key element of Flash is interactivity. This allows the user not only to view a Flash movie but also to interact with it.

Interactivity in Flash is created by assigning certain values and properties to buttons and text boxes so that one action triggers another, predefined one. This opens up numerous possibilities for Flash movies:

- Buttons can have action commands assigned to them

- Buttons can have actions that play sounds at certain points in the movie

- Buttons can be programmed to jump automatically to another part of the same movie

- Buttons can be used to open up other pages on the Web

- Buttons can be used to create a Menu bar

Creating interactive elements in a Flash movie is one of the more complex areas of the program. It is important to feel comfortable with the rest of the program before you begin using interactive functions. See Chapter Ten for more information on interactivity.

Obtaining Flash

Flash is produced by Macromedia and detailed information about the program can be found on their website at www.macromedia. com/software/flash.

This contains general information about the program, demos of how it works and links to sites that use Flash.

This is the Flash MX Home Page on the Macromedia site. Click here to download the program

To download a 30-day, fully functioning trial version of the program, click

here:

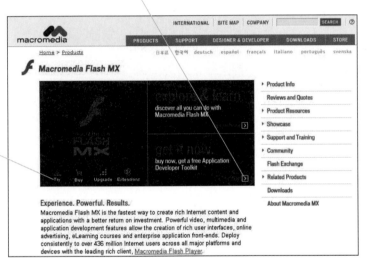

You can also buy the program from computer shops and software retailers. The price is approximately £240 and this includes disks for the PC and the Mac formats.

The Flash Player

In order to view a Flash movie on the Web, the Flash Player has to be installed on the user's computer. This is a plug-in application that allows the user to see the Flash movie playing. The Player is installed automatically when you install the full authoring program of Flash. However, if you want to view Flash-enabled Web pages before you buy the program then you will have to download the Player. This can be done from the Flash Home Page at www. macromedia.com/software/flashplayer/.

As Flash becomes more popular on the Web, so more and more browsers have the Player pre-installed. It has been estimated that 96% of Web users can view Flash without having to download the Player. However, always include a link for downloading the Player, just to be on the safe side.

Installing Flash

If you are installing Flash by downloading it from the Macromedia website, or from a CD-ROM, the process is similar. When the program begins to run, the Flash MX Installer icon will appear. Double-click on this to go to the Flash introduction window. Click OK and then follow the step-by-step instructions that take you through the installation process. Flash will set up folders on your hard drive for the program and, unless you have a good reason not to, it is best to install the program files here.

There is virtually no difference between the PC format of Flash and the Mac one. Any differences will be noted as and when they occur.

System requirements

The system requirements for Flash MX have to take into consideration the authoring program and also the Flash Player for viewing the end results.

Windows authoring

- 200 MHz Pentium processor

- Windows 98 SE or later

- 64 Mb of RAM (128 Mb recommended)

- 85 Mb of disk space

- 16-bit colour monitor capable of 1024 x 768 resolution

- CD-ROM drive

Versions of the Flash Player have been developed so that Flash content can be played over a variety of devices, including hand-held computers and mobile phones.

Mac authoring

- Power Mac or iMac with OS 9.1 or later or OS X version 10.1 or later

- 64 Mb of RAM (128 Mb recommended)

- 85 Mb of available disk space (ROM)

- 16-bit colour monitor capable of 1024 x 768 resolution

- CD-ROM drive

The Flash environment

Once Flash has been installed, it can be opened by double-clicking the Flash icon that the installation process should have placed on the Desktop (Windows) or in the Applications folder within the Finder (Mac).

The first view

When Flash is first opened, a new, blank document will be displayed on screen. This is the Flash authoring environment and it contains the elements that are needed to create a Flash movie. At first sight, it can seem a bit overwhelming, but each item has an important part to play in the authoring process:

Help can be obtained for elements of Flash by selecting Window>Answers from the Menu bar. This provides comprehensive Help information and also a link to the Macromedia website for latest information about Flash MX.

The Tools panel holds all of the main tools for creating and editing objects in Flash.

The Properties Inspector is a new feature in Flash MX and it displays the properties of a tool from the Tools panel or a selected object on the Stage.

Menu bar

Standard Toolbar (Windows only)

Layers section (adds different layers to a movie)

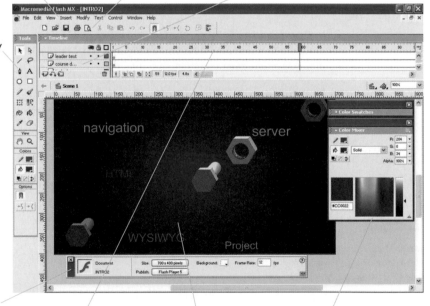

The Timeline (specifies how the movie is played)

The Stage (the content for each movie is placed here)

The Panels. These display information about items within a Flash movie

Getting started

This chapter looks at the elements that make up the Flash authoring environment. These include the means for controlling the content of a movie, the area where movies are created, and the toolbars, menus and panels that are used during the editing process.

Covers

The Timeline | 16

The Stage | 17

Tools and toolbars | 20

The Menu bar | 21

Properties Inspector | 22

Panels | 23

Viewing options | 24

QuickStart templates | 25

Accessibility | 27

Chapter Two

The Timeline

The Timeline is the section of Flash that enables you to organise all of the elements that make up your movie and see what is placed at certain points throughout your publication. The Timeline organises items such as scenes, layers and frames and it is also used to create animated effects. Of all of the elements of Flash, the Timeline is probably the most important and also the most complicated for the novice as there is no equivalent in other software packages.

If you want to create more space on the Stage for editing purposes, you can hide the Timeline. Select View from the Menu bar and click on Timeline so that there is no tick next to it. To make the Timeline reappear, reverse the process so the tick is showing.

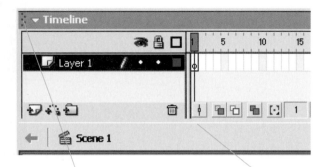

The Timeline offers several powerful organisational functions

Click and drag here to reposition the Timeline

Click and drag here to resize the Timeline

Layers are a very versatile way to control content while you are editing Flash movies. They are discussed in greater detail in Chapter Eight.

Elements of the Timeline:

Layers   Layer controls   Playhead   Frames   Frame rate

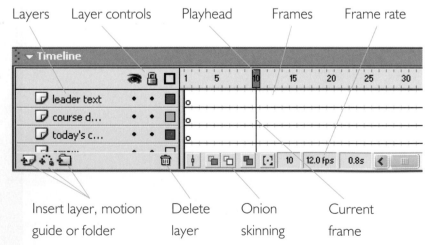

Insert layer, motion guide or folder

Delete layer

Onion skinning

Current frame

The Stage

The Library is an area for storing reusable items in a movie. This is looked at in greater detail in Chapter Six.

To edit a Flash file, make sure you open the authoring-format file rather than the movie-format one. If you open the movie one it will display the movie as it will appear when it is published and you will not be able to edit it. Authoring files have a .FLA file extension and this icon:

Movie files have a .SWF extension and this icon:

The Stage is the area where the content for a Flash movie is placed. This can be done by drawing objects directly onto the Stage, dragging them from the Flash Library or importing them from other applications. At any given frame in a Flash movie, the contents for that frame are displayed on the Stage. So the contents for frame 1 could look very different from the contents of frame 20 in a movie. The grey area around the Stage is known as the Work Area and this can be used to place animated objects that appear or disappear from the edge of the Stage. Only items that are visible within the Stage area will appear in the final movie.

Current scene

Drag the Playhead to move between frames. The content for each one covered will be displayed on the Stage

Edit scene

Edit symbols

The Stage, showing the content for the current frame (in this case, frame 1)

The Work Area. Items placed here will not appear in the final movie but it can be a starting or ending point for items that move on or off the Stage. To hide/show the Work Area, select View>Work Area

Document Properties dialog box

There are a number of settings that can be applied to the Stage and these are accessed through the Document Properties dialog box:

1   Select Modify>Document from the Menu bar

2   Various settings can be applied through the Document Properties dialog box

Stage dimensions

The default frame rate may not be the actual rate at which a movie is played on the user's browser. This is because they may have an older browser or a slower modem, so they cannot download the frames quickly enough. It could also be caused by certain parts of a movie being very processor-intensive.

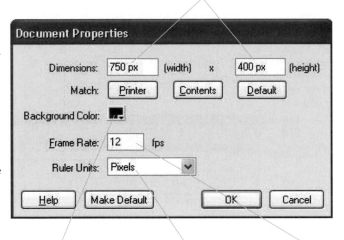

Background colour   Ruler settings   Frame rate

The settings in the Document Properties dialog box affect a Flash movie as follows:

•   *Frame Rate.* This is the speed, in frames per second, at which the movie is set to play. The default setting is 12

•   *Stage Dimensions.* This specifies the size at which the Stage is displayed

•   *Ruler settings.* This specifies the unit of measurement for all affected items on the Stage

•   *Background.* This specifies the background colour for the movie

The Stage colour will act as the default background for the whole of a movie. If the colour is changed at any point in the movie this will be reflected in the rest of the file too.

The Stage grid

It is possible to superimpose a grid over the Stage, to enable exact positioning and sizing of objects that are placed there. The grid is only visible in the authoring environment and it does not appear in the final, published movie.

Rulers can also be displayed on the Stage, by selecting View>Rulers from the Menu bar.

1   To display the grid on the Stage, select View>Grid>Show Grid from the Menu bar

2   To select the grid settings, select View>Grid>Edit Grid from the Menu bar

3   Select a colour for the grid by clicking here and selecting a colour from the palette that appears

Make sure there is a good contrast between the colour of the grid and the Stage background. Otherwise the grid will not be clearly visible, which rather defeats the purpose of having it there.

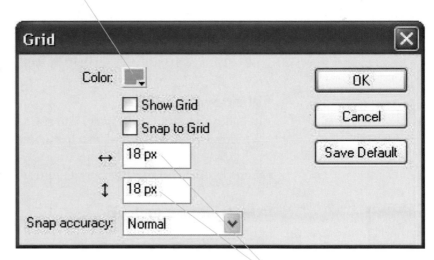

4   Select the spacing for the grid lines by entering it here. The measurement value is the same as in the Ruler Units box

Tools and toolbars

The Flash tools and toolbars are collections of buttons that offer quick access to several of the editing and drawing functions within the program. The tools and toolbars differ slightly between the Windows and the Mac versions of Flash:

Mac tools

The tools in the Tools panel are looked at in more detail in Chapter Three.

The Mac version of Flash MX consists only of the Tools panel and the Controller toolbar. The Tools panel contains all of the tools required to draw objects in Flash and the Controller toolbar is used to play through a movie while it is being edited in the authoring environment.

The Mac tools are accessed by selecting Window>Tools (for the Tools panel) or Window>Controller

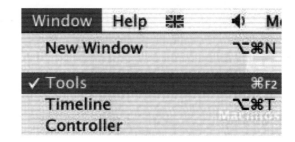

Windows toolbars

In addition to the Tools panel and the Controller toolbars, the Windows version of Flash also has a Standard toolbar and a Status bar. These are accessed by selecting View from the Menu bar and then checking on the appropriate option.

The Standard toolbar has icons that act as shortcuts for commonly used items on the Menu bar, such as Open, New, Save and Print. The Status bar denotes whether Caps Lock and Num Lock are on.

The Standard toolbar:

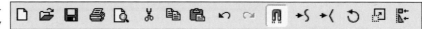

The Status bar:

The Menu bar

The Menu bar provides access to the core elements of Flash for editing movies. This is located at the top of the program and covers all of the functions that are required to create, edit and test a Flash movie.

The File menu

This contains menus for basic functions such as opening and saving movies and setting preferences for editing and publishing.

The Edit menu

This contains commands for editing items within a movie (e.g. Copy and Paste, selection tools and inserting objects).

The Mac version of Flash MX has a Flash menu which contains commands for Preferences, Keyboard Shortcuts, Font Mapping, Services and for hiding and quitting the program. The most important of these is the Preferences command.

The View menu

This gives you control of how your movie looks on screen. This includes showing and hiding items and viewing movies at different magnifications.

The Insert menu

This allows you to manipulate objects, layers and frames.

The Modify menu

This is used to access dialog boxes affecting the properties of items such as layers, scenes and the whole movie. It also provides for some general formatting.

The Text menu

This provides options for formatting text.

Menus that only apply to specific items are also available in Flash. These are known as contextual menus. These menus can be accessed by moving the cursor over the item whose contextual menu you want to see. Then right-click (Windows) or Ctrl+click (Mac) and the menu connected with that item will appear.

The Control menu

This lets you test your movie to see how various parts of it, or the whole thing, will look when it is played back.

The Window menu

This determines how the open windows are displayed, gives access to the Panels and, on the Mac, gives access to the Tools panel.

The Help menu

This provides online help and also the Flash help topics, lessons and samples.

Properties Inspector

In Flash MX a lot of the panels for creating content have been consolidated within the Properties Inspector. This is activated whenever a tool is selected from the Tools panel or an object is selected on the Stage. The Properties Inspector then displays the available options for the selected item.

Properties Inspector for tools

The Properties Inspector changes depending on the element that is selected. It can be used to display the properties of a variety of elements including drawing objects, movie clips, buttons and frames.

1 Select a tool from the Tools panel

2 The available options are displayed in the Properties Inspector

Properties Inspector for objects

1 Select an object on the Stage

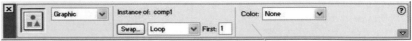

2 The available options are displayed in the Properties Inspector

Panels

Panels provide a variety of tools and options for creating and manipulating content. In Flash MX there are fewer panels than in previous versions of the program, as the Properties Inspector has taken over the same role for several tools and functions. The panels can be selected from the Window menu on the Menu bar. Once panels have been accessed, there are various ways in which to work with them.

Working with panels

The individual panels can be accessed by selecting Window from the Menu bar and then the required panel. The main panels are Align, Color Mixer, Color Swatches, Info, Scene and Transform.

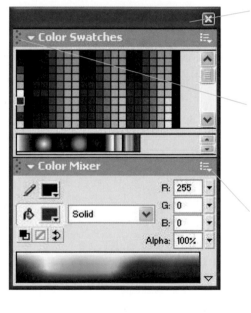

1 Drag the Title bar to move a panel around the Stage

2 Click here to drag a panel and group it with another, or break it apart from a group

3 Click here to access a panel menu:

4 Click here to expand or collapse a panel

5 Click here to close a panel

Viewing options

During the editing process it is important to be able to view the contents of the Stage at different magnifications. On some occasions you will want to zoom in on objects to edit them or position them precisely, while on others you will want to view the entire Stage in order to see how various elements appear in relation to others. This can be done by using either the View menu or the Zoom tool.

View menu

This allows you to select various magnification levels for viewing the Stage:

On the magnification menu, Show Frame displays the objects on the Stage and Show All displays the objects on the Stage and the Work Area, at the most appropriate size.

1 Select View > Magnification from the Menu bar

2 Select a magnification size

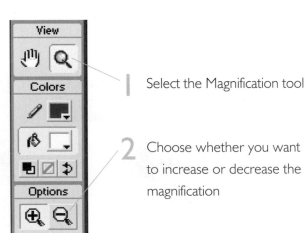

25%	
50%	
100%	Ctrl+1
200%	
400%	
800%	
Show Frame	Ctrl+2
Show All	Ctrl+3

Zoom tool

This can be used to magnify a certain part of the Stage.

The magnification can also be altered by clicking on the box next to the Symbol and Scene icons, at the right-hand side above the Stage, and selecting a magnification value.

1 Select the Magnification tool

2 Choose whether you want to increase or decrease the magnification

QuickStart templates

A new feature in Flash MX is the QuickStart Templates. These are a series of templates that have been created with a lot of the Flash functionality already added. They can then be customised to include your own content and they are an excellent option for quickly producing high-quality movies. To use QuickStart Templates:

1 Select File>New From Template from the Menu bar

2 Select a template and click on Create

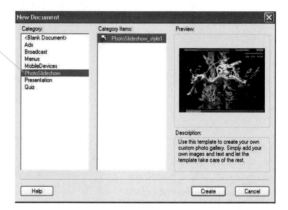

3 The template contains an instructions layer to help you add content. This can be deleted and is not visible in a published movie (below)

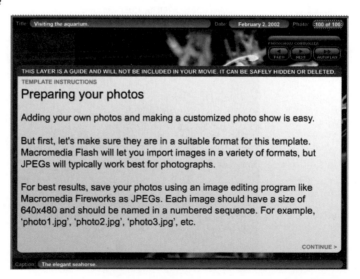

4 Enter content for the movie, using the Stage, layers and the Timeline

 The PhotoSlideshow template is a good way to add a bit of style to a presentation of a large number of photographic images.

 The QuickStart templates also have options for creating Flash content for mobile devices such as the Nokia Communicator.

5 When the movie is published, the template features, such as movie control buttons, can be used

Accessibility

An increasingly important issue for websites and Web designers is the one of accessibility. This concerns the use of the Web by blind or partially-sighted users. Despite the visual nature of the Web, this group of users can still access the information by using a form of technology that reads the content on screen. This means that someone who is blind or partially-sighted is provided with an audio version of the site they are viewing, rather than a visual one. This has a significant impact on the people creating websites, as they have to try and make sure that sites are compatible with the guidelines for accessibility readers.

Due to its very visual nature, it has been difficult in the past to provide textual descriptions for Flash movies. However, that has changed with Flash MX and it is now possible to add a textual description to a whole movie or to elements within a movie.

Making a movie accessible

When a whole movie is made accessible, a textual description is provided to let the user know the content of the movie or its function. To do this:

Accessibility is becoming an increasingly important issue for Web designers, particularly for websites that offer a public service. There have been some cases concerning possible legal action against organisations whose websites are not accessible for disabled users.

Macromedia has a site covering accessibility issues, which can be found at www. macromedia.com/ software/Flash/ productinfo/ accessibility/.

1 Make sure that nothing is selected on the Stage and click here on the Properties Inspector

2 Tick Make Movie Accessible so the movie can be read by an accessibility reader

3 Enter a name for the movie and a description. This will be read by the reader

Making elements of a movie accessible

A more involved option than providing a general description for a whole movie is to make elements accessible within a movie. This results in the accessibility reader providing an audio description for the various elements of a movie as it plays. Not all Flash objects are suitable for this and only the following ones can have accessibility descriptions applied to them:

- Text

- Input text fields

- Buttons

- Movie Clips

Even if the individual elements of a movie are made accessible, it may be of little use to someone who is blind or partially-sighted. It may be more effective to include a textual description for the whole movie and include an option that can be accessed to move to another document such as a HTML Web page.

To make these elements accessible in a movie:

1 Select one of the four elements described above

2 Click here on the Properties Inspector

3 Tick Make Object Accessible so the element can be read by an accessibility reader

4 Enter a name for the element and a description that will be used by the accessibility reader

Creating objects

This chapter looks at the basics of drawing objects in Flash and gives an overview of the contents of the Tools panel.

Covers

Stage and overlay objects | 30

Tools panel | 34

Line tool | 35

Pen tool | 36

Subselect tool | 37

Oval tool | 38

Rectangle tool | 39

Pencil tool | 40

Brush tool | 42

Ink Bottle tool | 43

Paint Bucket tool | 44

Dropper tool | 45

Eraser tool | 46

Chapter Three

Stage and overlay objects

One of the most powerful elements of Flash is its drawing tools. At first sight these may seem as if they are capable of little more than creating a variety of lines and shapes, such as circles and squares. However, these tools are a lot more versatile than this and, with practise and a small degree of artistic flair, they can be used to create an array of stunning graphical images. Before you get started with creating objects with the drawing tools there are a few areas to look at that have a major impact on drawing operations in Flash.

Overlay objects are created by grouping together two or more drawing objects. For instance, if you have created an image of a wall with dozens of rectangles as the bricks, this can be grouped together to make a single item. This is done by selecting Modify>Group from the Menu bar. Once objects have been grouped together they become a single overlay object.

Overlay objects can also be created by converting graphics into 'symbols'. This is discussed in greater detail in Chapter Six.

Stage level and overlay level objects

Simple objects are created in Flash with one of the drawing tools on the Stage. At this point they are in their most basic form and are known as 'stage level objects' i.e. they are placed directly on the Stage. However, it is also possible to convert objects into 'overlay level objects'. This in effect places them on a transparent film just above the Stage. To the naked eye, a stage level object and an overlay level object are identical. However, they both act differently within the Flash environment:

- Stage level objects are more versatile for editing purposes

- Stage level objects always reside on the Stage and they are covered by anything that is placed on top of them

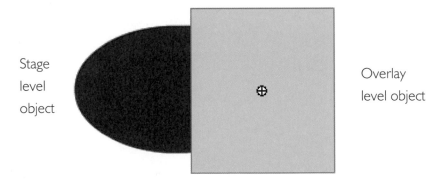

Stage level object

Overlay level object

Within the same layer, overlay level objects will always cover stage level ones.

If you want to convert an overlay level object back to a stage level one, perhaps for editing purposes, select the object then Modify>Break Apart from the Menu bar.

- Stage level objects can interact with each other, i.e. one stage level object can be placed over another similar object and, if the first one is moved, the covered portion of the second object is then cut away:

Draw two stage level objects, with parts of them overlapping

2 Select the Arrow tool and click and drag to select part of both objects

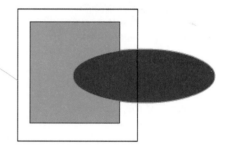

Several stage level objects can overlap on the Stage without affecting each other, if they are created on separate layers. Layers are looked at in greater detail in Chapter Eight.

3 Drag away the selected portion. This interaction between shapes can only be done with stage level objects. Since overlay level objects reside on a different level they do not actually 'touch' stage level ones

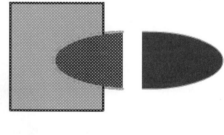

- Stage level objects are usually used when creating new graphics, while overlay level ones are used for the final version of the image

Strokes and fills

Solid objects drawn in Flash, such as circles and squares, are created by using an outline and a fill. In Flash terminology, these are known as strokes and fills respectively. Strokes and fills can be specified before a shape is created, or they can be edited at any time during the creation of the movie. Both stage level and overlay level objects can have their strokes and fills edited independently of each other.

Various drawing tools can be used to create and edit strokes and fills and these will be looked at throughout this chapter.

Fills can be plain colours, shades or even coloured lines to create a rainbow effect. These special effects can be particularly useful when creating buttons that the user will press to trigger an interactive function within a movie.

An object with a plain colour fill and the default stroke – a solid black line with a weight of 1

By changing the fill and stroke attributes, the object is changed considerably

If the fill of a stage level object is selected, it appears shaded. If the stroke is selected it appears as a thick striped line.

The stroke of an oval stage level object can be selected by clicking exactly on it once. However, only one side of a rectangular stage level object can be selected at a time.

To select all sides, select one side, then hold down Shift and select the other three. Or double-click on one side.

Selecting stage level and overlay level objects

Techniques for selecting objects will be looked at in the next chapter but there is one important point to make about selecting solid objects such as circles and squares:

- Overlay level objects can be selected by clicking on them once. The object then appears with a solid outline around it. The whole object can then be moved by clicking and dragging

An overlay object that has been selected. The whole object can now be moved by clicking and dragging

- Stage level objects are selected by clicking on either the stroke or the fill of the object. This can then be moved in the same way as above, except that only the selected element will move, i.e. either the stroke or the fill. If you want to move the whole of a stage level object, the stroke and the fill have to be selected together. This can be done by clicking above and to the left of the object and drawing a rectangle around the object so that it is all selected. It can then be moved by clicking and dragging

A stage level object selected by dragging with the Arrow tool from the top left of the object. The whole object can now be moved by dragging. (This is also how stage level objects are grouped)

Tools panel

All graphics created with the drawing tools are vector-based graphics. This means they are formed by mathematical equations rather than coloured dots (pixels). This gives images a smoother appearance and they retain their original quality if they are resized.

The Tools panel contains all of the tools needed to create graphics in Flash and they correspond to what you might find in an artist's studio: brushes, pencils, erasers and colour palettes. The Tools panel has options to enhance individual tools, such as line straightening with the Arrow tool. In addition the Properties Inspector can also be used to modify the selection made on the Tools panel e.g. the Line Tool Properties Inspector can be used to select the line style, weight and colour of the Line, Oval, Rectangle and Pencil tools.

The functions of the Text tool are dealt with separately, in Chapter Five.

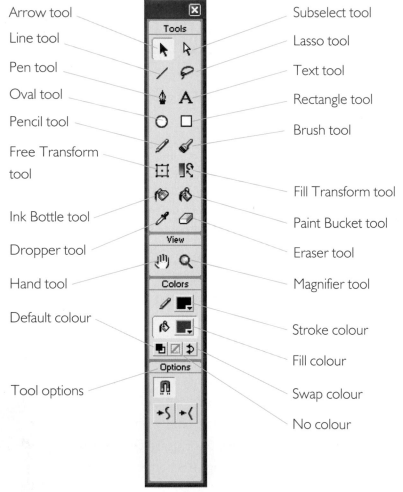

Arrow tool

Line tool

Pen tool

Oval tool

Pencil tool

Free Transform tool

Ink Bottle tool

Dropper tool

Hand tool

Default colour

Tool options

Subselect tool

Lasso tool

Text tool

Rectangle tool

Brush tool

Fill Transform tool

Paint Bucket tool

Eraser tool

Magnifier tool

Stroke colour

Fill colour

Swap colour

No colour

Line tool

The Line tool can be used to draw either straight or diagonal lines. It has no options but the line colour, style and weight can all be set in the Line Tool Properties Inspector:

1 Select the Line tool

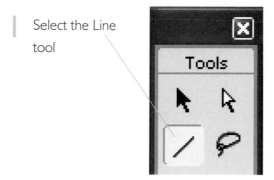

2 In the Properties Inspector click here for the Line Style options

3 Click here for the Line Color options

4 Click here for the Line Thickness options. This uses a sliding scale to increase the thickness of the line – the first option is Hairline and it is the thinnest line that can be used

5 Once you have chosen your options for a line, it can be drawn on the Stage by clicking and dragging. (The Line tool can be used to create either straight or diagonal lines)

Pen tool

The Pen tool works in the same way as the Pen tool in other Macromedia programs such as Freehand and Fireworks.

The Pen tool creates lines and curves but it does so by creating precise paths with specific points that allow for precise editing. The Pen tool has no options.

There are preferences for the Pen tool which can be set by selecting Edit>Preferences>Editing (Windows) or Flash>Preferences>Editing (Mac) from the Menu bar. The preferences are:

- *Show Pen Preview, which displays a preview of the line segment as you move the cursor around the Stage*
- *Show Solid Points, which displays selected points on a line as hollow and unselected ones as solid*
- *Show Precise Cursors, which displays the Pen cursor as a crosshair, for greater drawing accuracy*

Drawing a straight line with the Pen tool

1 Select the Pen tool and click and drag on the Stage. The point where you start dragging becomes the centre point

2 The two points at the ends of the line are known as anchor points

Drawing a curved line with the Pen tool

When the Pen tool is selected it will continue to add lines to the ones that have previously been drawn. To finish drawing a particular line and move onto another, double-click at the point where you want the line to stop.

1 Draw a straight line as above. With the Pen tool still selected click one of the anchor points and drag in the opposite direction to where you want the curve

2 The curve is created according to length and the degree to which the anchor points are dragged

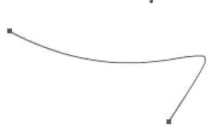

Subselect tool

The Subselect tool is used primarily in conjunction with the Pen tool, but it can also be used to edit lines created with the Pencil, Brush, Line, Oval and Rectangle tools. The Subselect tool has no modifiers and its main use is to edit lines that have been created as paths.

Creating a curved path from a straight line

Using the Subselect tool to select and edit lines can give greater accuracy and versatility than trying to do the same thing with the Arrow tool.

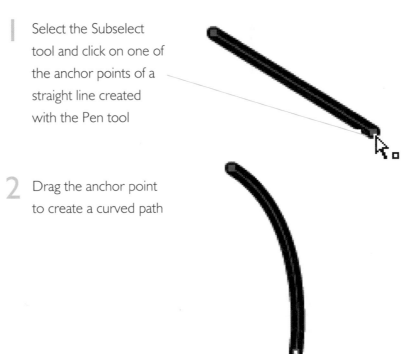

1   Select the Subselect tool and click on one of the anchor points of a straight line created with the Pen tool

2   Drag the anchor point to create a curved path

3   To revert to a straight line, reverse the process

The Subselect tool can also be used to modify enclosed shapes, such as rectangles and ovals, or shapes that have been created with the Pen tool.

Oval tool

This is similar to the Line tool in that it has no options of its own and the line style, weight and colour can be determined in the Line Tool Properties Inspector. In addition the fill for an oval can be selected from the Oval Tool Properties Inspector:

 To draw perfect circles, hold down the Shift key while dragging with the Oval tool crosshair.

Click here to select the Oval tool

Creating outline and solid ovals

By default, ovals are created with both a line around them and a fill. However, it is possible to create them with only one of these attributes:

 Once the attributes for a particular drawing tool have been set, they become the default settings for all of the other applicable drawing tools.

1 To create an outline oval, click the Fill Color button on the Properties Inspector

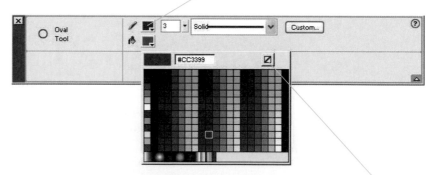

2 In the colour swatch that appears, click here to set the fill colour to 'no colour'. When the oval is drawn it will only have a line and no fill

Rectangle tool

The Rectangle tool can be used to draw rectangles and squares. It is similar to the Oval tool, except it has one option, for adding rounded corners to a rectangle:

To draw a perfect square, hold down Shift while you are dragging on the Stage with the Rectangle tool.

1 Select the Rectangle tool and click here to access the Rectangle Settings dialog box

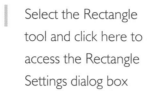

2 Enter a value here to specify how rounded you require the corners of a Rectangle to be

Rectangles can be created with only a stroke or only a fill, in exactly the same way as with ovals on the facing page.

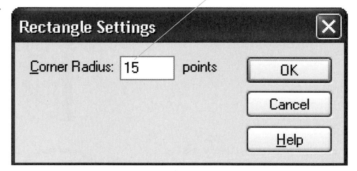

3 Select OK and then drag out the rectangle on the Stage

Pencil tool

The Pencil tool is a freehand drawing tool that can be used to create patterns, such as curved lines, or objects such as squares and circles. However, as with most freehand tools in drawing programs, creating objects with the Pencil tool can be an erratic and jerky experience – but only if it is used without any of the assistance that Flash provides for this particular tool. This assistance allows you to specify whether you want your freehand image to be straightened, smoothed or left as it is, with only minor amendments.

The Pencil tool does not have any other options, but the line style, weight and colour can be selected in the Pencil Tool Properties Inspector in the same way as for the Line tool.

Creating lines with the Pencil tool

When any line is drawn there will be a slight change in its appearance immediately after it has been finished. This is due to Flash ensuring that the finished line will appear as smooth as possible when viewed in the final movie.

| | Select the Pencil tool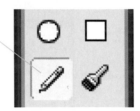

2 Draw a freehand shape on the Stage

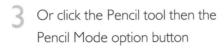

Shape recognition works best with the Straighten option selected. If the Smooth option is selected then you could end up with a rectangle with rounded edges. With Ink mode selected, there will be no shape recognition.

Pencil Mode Ink mode does not apply any straightening or smoothing and reproduces the line as it is drawn.

3 Or click the Pencil tool then the Pencil Mode option button

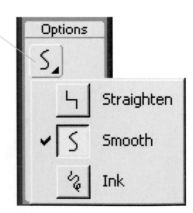

4 Now select either the Straighten or Smooth option to enable the Pencil tool to automatically straighten or smooth any lines that are drawn

Shape recognition only works when drawing circles, ovals and rectangles. If you try to draw a shape such as a triangle, the Pencil tool will try to either straighten or smooth it depending on which settings have been chosen. However, it will not necessarily transform it into a perfect triangle.

Using shape recognition

Not only does the Pencil tool straighten or smooth lines, it can also interpret a particular shape you are trying to draw and create a perfect version of it. This can be invaluable if you are trying to draw items such as ovals and rectangles.

Without shape recognition

Shape recognition applied

Setting assistance levels

There are various options that determine the level of assistance given to the drawing tools. Select Edit>Preferences>Editing (Windows) or Flash>Preferences>Editing (Mac):

- *Connect lines* determines how close the end lines of a rectangle or oval have to be before Flash closes them

- *Smooth curves* determines the degree by which curves are smoothed

- *Recognize lines* determines the tolerance for a line before it is automatically straightened

- *Recognize shapes* sets the tolerance before a shape is turned into an oval or a rectangle

- *Click accuracy* sets the accuracy for selecting strokes

Brush tool

The Brush tool creates broad brush strokes that give the effect of lines being created by actual paintbrushes.

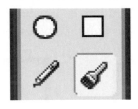

The brush modes that can be selected for the Brush tool are:

* *Paint Normal, which paints over everything on the selected level*
* *Paint Fills, which paints over fills but not lines*
* *Paint Behind, which paints behind objects*
* *Paint Selection, which paints inside a selected item, and;*
* *Paint Inside, which paints the fill of an item but not the line*

Brush tool options:

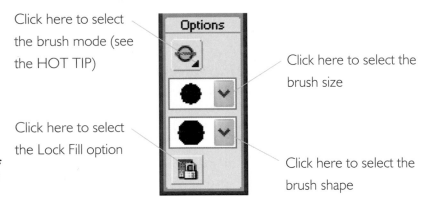

Click here to select the brush mode (see the HOT TIP)

Click here to select the Lock Fill option

Click here to select the brush size

Click here to select the brush shape

To use the Brush tool, draw a shape on the Stage as if you were using a paintbrush or a thick crayon. Click and drag to create a line with the Brush tool. You can release the mouse and then draw another line: as long as it is touching the first line, and is the same colour, it will become part of the same shape. This way you can build up complex shapes using a variety of lines. You can even change the brush size and shape halfway through and the new lines will become part of the original object, as long as they are touching it. Brush strokes are objects rather than true strokes.

While you are using the Brush tool it may appear that it is covering everything on the Stage. However, when you finish using the tool the result will take on the attributes of the selected brush mode.

The Lock Fill option can be used if you are using a gradient or a bitmap as a brush stroke fill. Select the Brush tool then select a gradient/bitmap. You can then draw separate shapes on the Stage and the fill will change in each one, giving the effect of the gradient/bitmap in a disjointed pattern.

Ink Bottle tool

The Ink Bottle tool can be used to add an outline (stroke) to an object that does not have one, or to change the attributes of an existing outline. This only applies to stage level objects. The line colour, weight and style can be selected in the Ink Bottle Tool Properties Inspector. There are no other options for the Ink Bottle tool.

To use the Ink Bottle tool:

1 Select the Ink Bottle tool and then select the required line colour, weight and style in the Ink Bottle Tool Properties Inspector

Ink Bottle attributes can be applied to outlines of elements within an object. However, the new line attributes will only be applied to any elements within the object that can support an outline. For instance, if you had a face graphic and clicked inside it with the Ink Bottle tool, elements such as the eyes, nose and mouth would have the selected outline attributes applied to them.

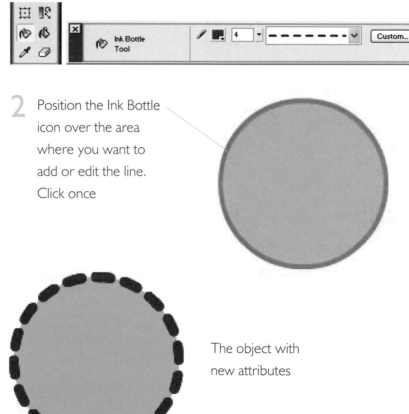

2 Position the Ink Bottle icon over the area where you want to add or edit the line. Click once

The object with new attributes

Paint Bucket tool

The Paint Bucket tool can be used to create a coloured fill within an object, or it can change an existing fill. The fill colour can be selected in the Paint Bucket Tool Properties Inspector:

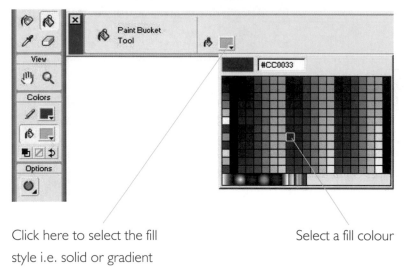

Click here to select the fill style i.e. solid or gradient

Select a fill colour

The only option for the Paint Bucket tool is the Gap Size:

Select a gap size (e.g. Don't Close Gaps stops a fill being applied to objects with gappy outlines)

To use the Paint Bucket tool, select a fill colour and position the bucket over the object to be filled or whose fill is to be edited. Click once to add the new fill:

Dropper tool

The Dropper tool only works on stage level objects and it allows you to take the fill or stroke attributes of one item and transfer them to another. It has no modifiers or Properties Inspector.

To use the Dropper tool:

If you want to transfer the stroke attributes from one object to another, click once on its outline with the Dropper tool. If you want to transfer the fill, then click once on that.

1 Select the Dropper tool and position it over the fill or stroke that you want to copy. Click once to load the Dropper tool

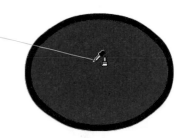

2 The Dropper tool then activates either the Paint Bucket tool or the Line tool, depending on whether the dropper was loaded with the fill or the stroke of an object

The Dropper tool can also be used to capture bitmap images so that they can be used as fills.

3 Click once on the selected object to transfer the fill or stroke from the original object

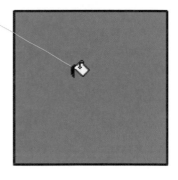

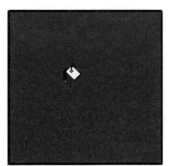

The object with the new fill

Eraser tool

The Eraser tool can be used to delete items on the Stage. It can be used on both strokes and fills, but it can only be applied to stage level objects.

When you are using the Eraser tool it may appear as if it is deleting everything it touches rather than following the specifications of the Eraser mode modifiers. However, when the mouse is released, only the specified elements will have been deleted. (Any other items will reappear.)

Eraser tool options:

Click here to select an Eraser Mode (see below)

Click here to select the Faucet

Click here then select an Eraser Shape

The Faucet option for the Eraser tool can be used to delete an entire outline or fill with a single click.

The options for Eraser Mode are:

- *Erase Normal*, which erases both strokes and fills

- *Erase Fills*, which only erases fills, even if the eraser passes over a stroke

- *Erase Lines*, which only erases strokes, even if the eraser passes over a fill

- *Erase Selected Fills*, which only erases fills that have first been selected. Everything else is untouched

- *Erase Inside*, which only erases inside an area without affecting the stroke

If the Eraser tool is applied to overlay level objects, it will have no effect.

Editing objects

This chapter looks at some of the editing functions that can be applied to drawing objects in Flash. It covers selecting items; editing lines; resizing and reshaping objects; aligning items; changing the stacking order; and creating cut-aways.

Covers

Selecting with the Arrow tool | 48

Selecting with the Lasso tool | 50

Grouping objects | 51

Free Transform tool | 52

Reshaping objects | 54

Aligning objects | 56

Pixel snapping | 57

Stacking order | 58

Cut-aways | 59

Paste in Place | 60

Chapter Four

Selecting with the Arrow tool

To select more than one segment of a line, hold down Shift and click on the segments you want to select. This is the default setting but it can be changed so that multiple segments can be selected just by clicking on them.

Selecting lines

Since lines in Flash are based on vectors (mathematical equations) rather than being composed of dots, it is possible to select different parts as well as the whole thing. This can be useful if you want to edit one specific part of a line. Lines drawn with the Line tool or the Pencil tool can be selected this way, but only if they are stage level objects. When a line is created in Flash the vector calculation creates a corner point and a curve point for each segment of the line. The curve point is between two corner points and this is the segment of a line that can be select by clicking on it. To select part of a line:

Although the Brush tool can be used to create what appear to be lines, these are in fact blocks of colour. You cannot select a segment by clicking on it. However, parts of brush stroke objects can be selected by clicking and dragging – see the facing page.

The Subselect tool can also be used to edit lines. To do this, click once on a line to select the whole line. Then click and drag on the markers that appear on the line to alter the appearance of it.

1 Select the Arrow tool; place it at the start of the line. This is the first corner point, shown by a right angle next to the cursor

2 Move the cursor along the line. A small curve will appear next to the cursor, denoting it is a curve point

3 When the cursor finds the next corner point the right angle reappears. This area is a line segment

4 Click once anywhere on the segment to select it

Selecting parts of objects

In addition to selecting complete objects and segments of lines, it is also possible to use the Arrow tool to select parts of an object. This can be useful if you want to edit a portion of an object:

Only stage level objects can have segments selected.

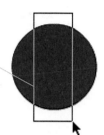

1. With the Arrow tool selected, click and drag to create the area within the object you want to edit

When clicking and dragging to select part of an object, position the cursor outside the object to begin the operation. Otherwise you may select the object's fill or outline.

2. The selected area can now be edited – for instance, changing its colour fill with the Paint Bucket or Brush tools

This technique can also be used to select parts of several different objects:

1. Click and drag to create the selection area

If selected objects are grouped they become a single item as an overlay level object.

2. The selected objects, or areas of objects, become shaded to indicate they are selected. They can then be edited, grouped or moved

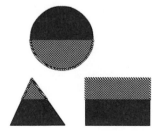

Selecting with the Lasso tool

While the Arrow tool can be used to select objects by clicking on them or drawing symmetrical boxes around them, the Lasso tool is better for selecting irregular shapes. This can be done by creating a freehand selection or one using the Polygon option.

Freehand selection

Selections made with the Lasso tool have to have the same starting and ending point.

1 Select the Lasso tool. The options do not have to be selected

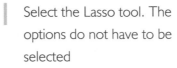

2 Trace around the object to be selected. Finish the selection by double-clicking at the point where you began the selection

When making a freehand selection, keep the mouse button pressed down until you want to finish the process.

Polygon selection

1 Select the Lasso tool and the Polygon option

2 Click on a starting point and drag out a line. Release the mouse button where you want the line to end. Repeat this until the whole shape is enclosed by these lines

Grouping objects

Groups are always overlay level objects, even if they are made up of only stage level ones.

Several individual objects can be grouped together to form a new, single object. Groups can consist of any objects on the Stage, including stage level objects, overlay level objects, bitmaps and text. Creating groups is useful for applying the same editing technique to multiple items simultaneously, such as moving or resizing.

To group objects:

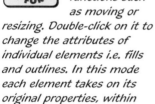

Click on a group once to select it for editing functions such as moving or resizing. Double-click on it to change the attributes of individual elements i.e. fills and outlines. In this mode each element takes on its original properties, within the group.

1 Use the Arrow tool to select the items you want to group, either by shift-clicking or by dragging and drawing around them

2 Select Modify>Group from the Menu bar

3 A blue border appears around the grouped objects

To ungroup an object, select it then select Modify>Ungroup from the Menu bar.

4 Double-click on the group to edit individual items within it. The other items on the Stage are greyed out and the group is identified here

Free Transform tool

The Free Transform tool can be used to perform several operations on objects, including resizing, rotating, skewing, distorting and enveloping. To use the Free Transform tool:

Objects can be resized by exact amounts by using the Info panel. To access this select Window> Info from the Menu bar and enter values in the H (height) and W (width) boxes to resize the selected object. An object's position can also be changed this way by entering values in the X and Y co-ordinates boxes.

Click here on the Tools panel and select an object on the Stage on which the Free Transform options will be applied. These options can be selected here on the Tools panel

Resizing

Click here on the Tools panel and resize the object by dragging one of the resizing handles

Rotating and skewing

An object can be rotated (moved to varying degrees around its centre point) or skewed (distorted at various angles along its horizontal or vertical axis). To do this:

Objects can quickly be rotated by set amounts by selecting Modify>Transform from the Menu bar and selecting Rotate 90° CW (clockwise); Rotate 90° CCW (counter-clockwise); Flip Vertical or Flip Horizontal.

Click here on the Tools panel and drag just outside a corner handle to rotate an object. Drag on a centre handle to skew the object

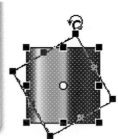

Distorting

Click here on the Tools panel and click and drag on one of the object handles to distort it

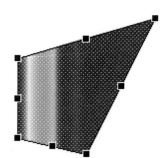

All of the functions of the Free Transform tool can be accessed from the Menu bar by selecting Modify>Transform and then choosing the required option. The Scale and Rotate option offers a dialog box for entering values but the others perform the function by dragging the object in the same way as using the Free Transform tool.

Envelope

The envelope function allows you to reshape an object using numerous points that are placed along its outline when this option is selected. To do this:

Click here on the Tools panel. The envelope points appear along the border of the object

Reshape the object by dragging the envelope points. This creates a similar effect to when the Pen tool is used, in that paths are created which can be reshaped by dragging anchor points

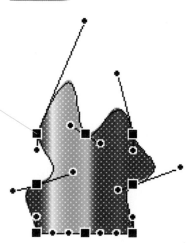

Reshaping objects

Both lines and fills can have their shapes altered, which can be a useful way of manipulating items and creating some interesting freehand effects. When reshaping objects there are three important points to remember:

- You can only reshape stage level objects

- When you are reshaping lines or fills you do not have to select them first. If you do you will move the item rather than reshape it

- Both lines and fills in Flash are made up of corner points and curve points. The corner points are at the end of lines or at a point in a line or fill that Flash calculates is at a sufficient angle. Corner points are denoted by a small right angle next to the cursor when it passes over one. These can be used to reshape the corner of fills or the end of lines. Curve points are denoted by a small curve next to the cursor. These can be used to reshape the middle of fills or lines.

Reshaping a straight line

In Flash, any points between the two corner points of a straight line are considered to be curve points, even though they are completely straight.

1   Select the Arrow tool and position it over one end of the line, without selecting the line. A small right angle will appear next to the cursor

2   Drag to stretch and reposition the line

Reshaping a curved line

| Select the Arrow tool and position it over part of the line, without selecting it. A small curve will appear next to the cursor

HOT TIP

It is possible to add corner points to fill objects. This gives increased flexibility when reshaping objects and means that corner points can even be added to objects such as perfect circles.

To create corner points: select the Arrow tool and position it over a curve point so the small curve is showing. Hold down Ctrl+click (Windows) or Alt+click (Mac) and then drag the cursor. As it is dragged the object will be reshaped and a new corner point will be created.

2 Drag to reshape the curve

Reshaping a fill

| Select the Arrow tool and position it over either a corner point or a curve point of the fill object

2 Click and drag to reshape the fill

Reshaping using corner points

Reshaping using curve points

Aligning objects

Even with the grid and ruler options, it can be useful to have a function for aligning a number of objects in one operation – for instance if you want to line up a group of buttons as navigation tools. Flash provides this with a number of alignment options for both stage level and overlay level objects.

Alignment panel

Alignment is done with the Align panel and there are a number of options that can be selected.

To align objects:

1 Select the objects to be aligned

In addition to aligning objects vertically and horizontally, the Align panel also has options for matching the width and height of the largest object in the selection.

2 Select Window>Align from the Menu bar

Text can be aligned using the same method as for objects.

3 Select the required alignment options

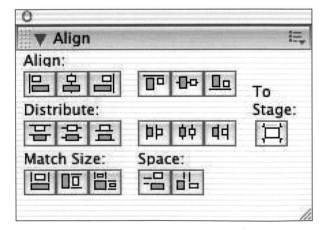

Pixel snapping

Pixel snapping is a function that can be used to align objects with great accuracy, as it aligns objects to individual pixels on the Stage.

To use pixel snapping:

1 Set the magnification to 400% or greater and make the Stage grid visible by selecting View>Grid> Show Grid from the Menu bar

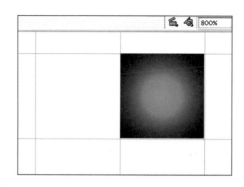

To hide the pixel grid, hold down the X key. Release it to view the grid again.

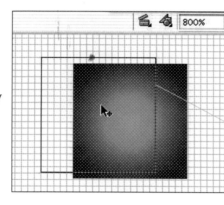

2 Turn on pixel snapping by selecting View>Snap to Pixels from the Menu bar

3 Reposition an object relative to the grid

4 Wherever else the object is positioned it will be in the same relative position on the pixel grid i.e. if it was placed between two grid squares, then its subsequent position will snap to the grid at this relative point

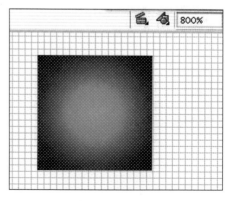

Stacking order

As movies are created, the number of objects on the Stage increases. This is generally not a problem if the objects are apart, but when they start to overlap it can become an issue. For instance, if you have an image of a person kicking a ball, it is important to have the ball showing in front of the individual rather than behind them. This is known as stacking, and Flash enables you to arrange objects in a variety of ways.

Only overlay objects can be arranged: if you have a stage level object that you want to arrange it has to first be grouped or turned into a symbol (see Chapter Six).

To arrange overlay level items:

You should note that the options for the Arrange menu are:

- *Bring to Front. This brings the selected object to the top of the stacked objects*
- *Move Forward. This brings the selected object forward one level*
- *Send Backward. This moves the selected object back one level*
- *Send to Back. This moves the selected object to the back of the stacked objects*
- *Lock. This locks the selected object in its current position so it cannot be moved, and;*
- *Unlock All. This unlocks any previously locked objects*

1 Select the object whose stacking order you want to change

2 Select Modify>Arrange from the Menu bar and select one of the stacking options (see the DON'T FORGET Tip)

3 The selected object is now at the back

Cut-aways

The reason stage level objects cannot be stacked is because they physically affect each other when one is placed on top of another. In this way, one stage level object can be used to create cut-aways from another. This can be done with either objects or lines.

Cut-aways with objects

1 Draw two stage level objects, one on top of the other

2 Select one object and click and drag it to see the cut-away effect

Cut-aways with lines

1 Draw a stage level object. With either the Line or the Pencil tool, draw a line across it. This divides the object into two distinct segments

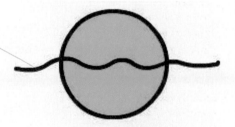

2 Select one of the segments and click and drag it to see the effect of the cut-away

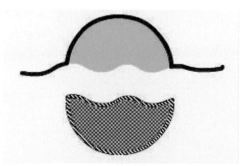

Paste in Place

In common with many software programs, Flash offers the standard Copy, Paste and Cut facilities. In addition, it has an option for pasting objects into the same relative position as they were copied from.

Using Paste in Place

To paste an object in the same relative position (measured from the top-left corner of the Stage) from where it was copied:

1 Select an object in the first frame of a movie and select Edit>Copy from the Menu bar

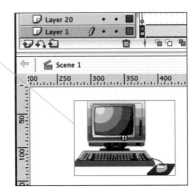

Paste in Place is an excellent option if you want to have various items in exactly the same place throughout a movie. This could include items such as company logos or menu bars.

2 Insert a new layer (or move to another frame) and select Edit>Paste in Place. The object is then pasted into exactly the same position as from where it was copied

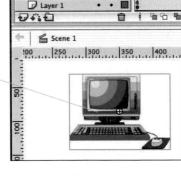

3 Drag the top object to view the duplicate underneath

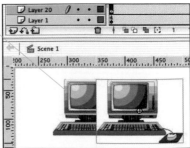

Colour and text

Both colour and text can be used to give extra dimension to a Flash movie. This chapter looks at adding colours and gradients to objects, creating new colours and gradients and selecting colours. It also shows how to add, format and manipulate text.

Covers

Standard Color palette | 62

Adding solid colours | 63

Adding gradients | 65

Fill Transform tool | 67

More colour options | 69

Selecting colours | 70

Adding text | 71

Formatting text | 73

Manipulating text | 74

Chapter Five

Standard Color palette

When the Color Line or Color Fill box is chosen for a drawing tool the standard Flash Color palette appears. This has a selection of the most commonly used colours and it contains two elements:

- *Solid colours.* Solid blocks of colour

- *Gradient colours.* Bands of colours that merge into each other to give a gradient effect. Gradient colours can either be radial gradients, which use rings of colours to create the gradient effect, or linear gradients, which use lines of colour

Any of the applicable drawing tools can be loaded with fill or gradient colours. Select the tool you want to use and then select an option from the Color palette. This will stay in place for any other drawing tools, until another selection is made.

Select a solid colour fill

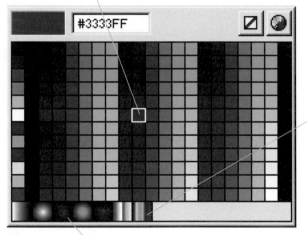

`#3333FF`

Select a linear gradient fill

Select a radial gradient fill

Radial gradients are excellent for items such as buttons on a Web page. The gradient gives the button greater depth and creates a more interesting 3-D effect.

Gradient types:

Solid colour fill

Linear gradient fill

Radial gradient fill

Adding solid colours

Since not everyone wants to be restricted to just the colours within the standard Color palette, Flash has an option for creating new colours and adding these to the Color palette. This gives an almost limitless range of colours from which to choose, but if these are intended for a Web page, it is worth remembering that they may not necessarily be displayed on the user's browser exactly as intended (see the tip).

Creating a new solid colour

The maximum number of colours guaranteed to be displayed correctly on a computer monitor is 256 (or only 216) and this is known as the Web Safe Color palette.

If you use colours outside this range some monitors will interpret them as best they can, but they may differ from the original. This is known as 'dithering' and it usually results in inferior colour representation. If in doubt, stick to Web Safe colours, which are the ones Flash uses by default.

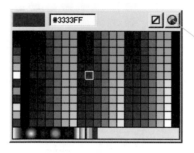

Click here on the Color palette to access the Color dialog box

2 On a Mac the Color Picker is activated. Do any of the following:

Drag slider(s) to select a colour

Colour preview

Select a colour model

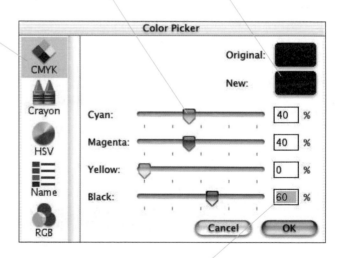

Create a colour by inserting values in the boxes

Hexadecimal is a system that uses six digits to denote colours. It works by giving values for red, green and blue, using a base system of sixteen. This uses the numbers 0–9 and the letters A–F. Each of the three colours (Red, Green and Blue) used to create a hexadecimal colour has a combination of two letters/digits assigned to it.. For instance, white is FFFFFF and black is 000000.

There are 256 (16x16) hexadecimal combinations, matching the Web Safe palette.

3 In Windows the Color dialog box appears. Do any of the following:

Edit hue/saturation by dragging the crosshair

Edit brightness by dragging the slider

Select a standard colour here

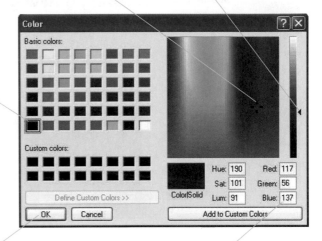

Click OK once a colour has been created

Create custom colours by entering values in these boxes

Creating colours with the Mixer panel

New colours can also be created by using the Mixer panel:

Any colour that is created in the Mixer panel is immediately applied as the fill colour or stroke colour (whichever is selected) on the Tools panel.

Enter values in the boxes for the amount of red, green and blue in the new colour

If the Alpha setting for a colour (its transparency) is at 100% then it will be at its most dense. If it is at 0% it will be completely transparent i.e. invisible.

Enter a value here for the level of transparency of the colour

Click here to select a new colour

Adding gradients

Gradients can be added and edited in a similar way to solid colours. This is done by accessing the Fill panel and selecting which colours will make up the gradient and how thick each band of colour will be.

In addition to accessing the Color palette by selecting a drawing tool and then selecting the Fill or Line Color box, it can also be displayed by selecting Window>Colors from the Menu bar.

Creating a new gradient:

1 Select Window>Color Mixer from the Menu bar

2 Select a linear or radial gradient

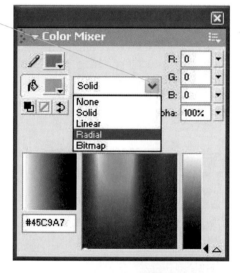

Gradients can produce very effective fills for items such as buttons. However, try not to overdo this effect and use gradients carefully.

3 The colours that make up the gradient are shown here. Click once on one of the pointers to edit a particular colour in the gradient. A new colour can be selected from the Color Swatches panel that appears

4 Drag the pointers to change the amount of each colour in the gradient. The effect is shown in the preview box

Colours can be removed from gradients by clicking and dragging a gradient pointer off the scale.

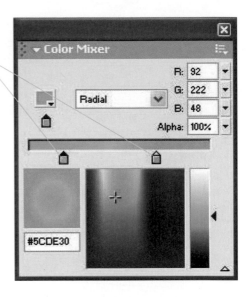

Gradients must have a minimum of two colours. If more colours are used this allows for either dramatic effects to be created with different colours or greater subtlety to be achieved by using several shades in the gradient.

5 Add more pointers by Shift-clicking at the bottom of the gradient colour bar. The more pointers, the more flexibility there is for editing the gradient

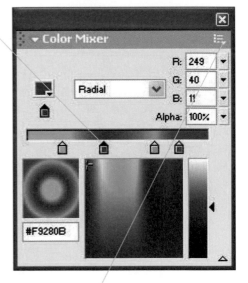

6 Click here and select Add Swatch to add the gradient to the Color Swatches panel

Fill Transform tool

Gradients can be applied to objects in the same way as solid colours: select a drawing tool such as the Oval or Rectangle tool, select the Fill box and choose a gradient from the Color palette. Alternatively, the Fill Transform tool can be used to change the gradient of an existing stage level object. It is also possible to use the Fill Transform tool to edit existing gradient fills.

Moving a gradient's centre point

1 Select the Fill Transform tool from the Tools panel

2 Select the object whose gradient you want to edit (three small buttons appear – see page 68)

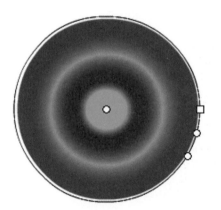

3 Click and drag the centre point to change the position of the gradient

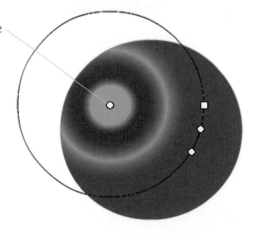

Changing a gradient's shape

1 Select the Fill Transform tool as on the previous page and select the object to be edited

2 Drag on the Change Gradient Shape button to make the gradient larger or smaller

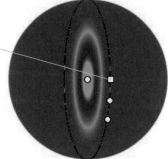

Changing a gradient's radius

1 Select the Fill Transform tool as above and select the object to be edited

2 Click and drag on the Change Gradient Radius button to make the gradient's radius larger or smaller

Changing a gradient's rotation

1 With the Fill Transform tool, select an object

2 Click and drag on the Change Gradient Rotation button to rotate the gradient (this has no effect unless its centre has already been moved or its shape changed)

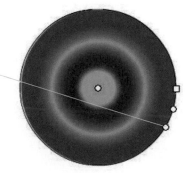

More colour options

Swapping colours

It is possible to swap the selected colours for the stroke and the fill options. To do this:

1 Click here on the Tools panel

2 The colours for the stroke
   and the fill
   options are
   automatically
   swapped

To access the Mixer panel, select Window>Color Mixer from the Menu bar.

Using the Mixer panel

Instead of having to use two separate routes each time you want to change the colour for the stroke and the fill options, they can both be changed at the same time using the Mixer panel:

Select the line colour or fill colour option and then select a colour for each one

Click here to make the colours black and white

Click here to select no colour

Click here to swap colours

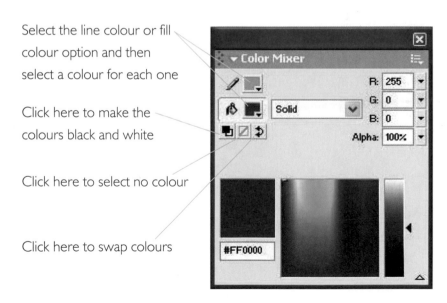

Selecting colours

Solid colours can be selected with the Arrow tool or the Lasso tool. However, this is not always effective if you want to select areas of colour within a bitmap image i.e. a photograph. To do this, the Lasso tool can be used in conjunction with its Magic Wand modifier:

1 Import an image and break it apart so that individual areas of colour can be selected (see the tip)

Bitmaps can be imported into Flash using the Import command on the Menu bar. Before the colours in a bitmap can be edited the image has to be broken apart. To do this, select the image then select Modify>Break Apart from the Menu bar.

Once an area of colour has been selected it can be recoloured, resized, rotated, moved or copied.

For more on working with bitmaps, see Chapter Seven.

2 Select the Lasso tool and the Magic Wand modifier

3 Select the Magic Wand Settings modifier and enter the relevant settings

4 Select an area of colour on the bitmap by clicking on it once with the Magic Wand tool

Adding text

In Flash, text can be more than just plain words on the screen. It can serve this purpose perfectly well, but it can also be used to create animations. These will be dealt with in Chapter Nine. However, it is important to look at the basics of text entry. Two points to remember:

- Text is created as an overlay level object, so it is placed on top of any stage level objects on the Stage

- In its original format, text is created in text labels or boxes. These can be edited and formatted in a similar way to text in a word processing program. However, text can also be broken apart so that individual words and letters can be used as shapes and formatted accordingly

The text options can also be selected from the Menu bar. Select Text and then either Font, Size, Style, Align or Tracking.

Text can be added as text labels or text boxes.

Adding a text label

Select the Text tool in the Tools panel, then select the following options as appropriate from the Text Tool Properties Inspector:

Click here to select a font

Click here to select a font size

In the Text Tool Properties Inspector there is an option box for kerning – in the slider which launches, select the amount of space between individual letters.

Click here to select tracking and character position

Click here to apply a colour

Click here to select Bold and/or Italic

2   Click on the Stage with the Text tool. Enter the text into the text label

Text labels can be used to position specific words at the end of a line. Press Return after the required word, and a new line will be started underneath it.

3   The text will continue

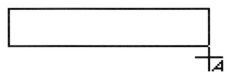

A text label will keep expanding

along the Stage, and eventually off the edge into the Work Area, unless Return is pressed to create a new line

To add a text box

1   Follow Step 1 on page 71

2   Click and drag the text crosshair on the Stage to create a text box of a specific width

A text label is denoted by a small circle in the top right hand corner of the box into which the text is typed. A text box is denoted by a small square.

3   When the text is entered it will wrap (move to the next line down) when it exceeds the width of the text box. The text will expand downwards, increasing the height of the text box, but the width will remain constant

Text in a text box will wrap downwards, expanding the box

Formatting text

General formatting

Text can be aligned in either a text label or a text box by inserting the cursor within a paragraph and selecting the Alignment options in the Text Tool Properties Inspector.

1   With the Text tool, select the text by clicking and dragging the cursor over it

2   Select options from the Text Tool Properties Inspector, as with creating text on page 71

3   The text displays the selected choices

Text is versatile

Paragraph formatting

For paragraph properties, line spacing is always measured in a default of points. The margin and indent measurements default to the settings applied to the ruler. This can be changed by selecting Modify>Movie and entering a new unit of measurement in the Ruler Units box.

1   Select the Paragraph panel by clicking the Format button on the Text Tool Properties Inspector

2   Enter settings in the Format Options dialog box

The amount the first line of the paragraph is indented

The amount of space between lines

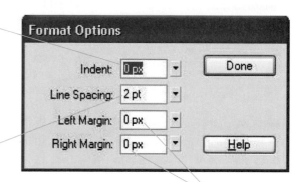

The left and right margin indents

Manipulating text

In addition to standard formatting for text, it can also be manipulated as if it were a graphic, rather than plain text.

Rotating and resizing

As with graphical objects, words or letters can be rotated and resized:

| With the Free Transform tool select a word or letter by clicking on it once

2 Click the Rotate modifier to rotate the text by clicking and dragging on a corner handle

or

Click the Resize modifier to resize the text by clicking and dragging one of the resizing handles

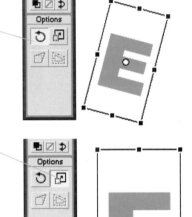

Reshaping text

Text can also be reshaped like a graphical object:

| Select a letter or word and select Modify > Break Apart from the Menu bar

2 Click and drag either a corner point or a curve point to reshape the text

Symbols and instances

Flash has a function for creating an object once and then using it numerous times, without significantly increasing the size of the movie file. The two items used for this are called 'symbols' and 'instances'. A symbol is a master object which can be reused numerous times to create copies (instances) on the Stage.

This chapter looks at creating and editing symbols and instances. It also looks at the Library, the area where symbols are stored.

Covers

Symbols and instances defined | 76

The Library | 78

Converting objects to symbols | 82

Creating a new symbol | 84

Symbol Editing Mode | 86

Editing symbols | 87

Editing instances | 88

Chapter Six

Symbols and instances defined

Whenever a symbol is created it is automatically placed in the Flash Library. This is an area for storing the items that are used in a particular movie – see pages 78–81.

Symbols and instances play a vital role in ensuring Flash's ability to create graphic-intensive movies, while still maintaining file sizes small enough to achieve an acceptably fast downloading time. Symbols are reusable items and they can consist of animations, static graphics, text or interactive buttons. An instance is created from a symbol and when it is placed on the Stage it appears identical to the symbol from which it was created. So an instance of a star graphic would look exactly like its symbol, at least when it is first placed on the Stage.

However, although instances look as if they are straight copies of the original symbols they are in fact only *references* to the symbol. This means they are not actually objects in their own right and so take up virtually no file space. So, a dozen instances could be created from one symbol and the amount of file space taken up would be only a little more than that occupied by the original symbol. This is invaluable if you want to use the same object numerous times in a movie. In addition, instances do not have to look exactly like the symbol from which they were created: it is possible to change their size and colour to give the effect of several different objects, while still referring them back to one original symbol.

Although individual instances can be edited independently of the original symbol and any other instances created from it, if the symbol is edited these changes will affect all of the instances of it on the Stage.

Six instances created from one symbol – each has been recoloured, resized or rotated but they all still refer back to the original symbol

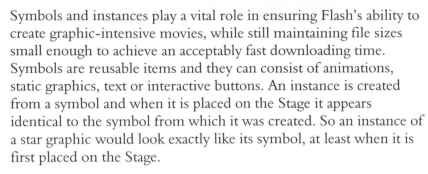

Types of symbols

There are three types of symbol, each of which can be used for certain functions. In addition, there are three other items that act in a similar way to symbols, even though they do not technically fall into this category:

Symbol types are also known as behaviors i.e. how the symbol reacts when it is placed in a movie.

- *Graphics.* These are the objects that are created with the Flash drawing tools. Not all graphics have to be turned into symbols and if it is an item that is only going to be used once, and remain static throughout the movie, then there is little point in changing it into a symbol. However, if a graphic is going to be reused throughout a movie, or even used in another movie, then it is worth turning it into a symbol. This operation is very quick and can save a lot of time and effort

Symbols have their own timelines that run independently of a movie's main Timeline. This is particularly important for button and movie clip instances since it gives them greater flexibility in the way they relate to the main movie i.e. a movie clip could be playing even though the main Timeline has stopped.

- *Buttons.* These are interactive objects that perform an action when they are pressed by the user. They can be programmed to perform a number of actions and these are looked at in detail in Chapter Ten

- *Movie clips.* These are animations that are placed within a movie. They are self-contained animated objects which can be used multiple times in a movie. Movie clips are a powerful and flexible way to create impressive animated effects and they are looked at in detail in Chapter Nine

- *Bitmaps, sounds and video.* Several types of bitmap images, sounds and video formats can be imported into Flash. They are then treated like symbols and the equivalent of instances can be created from them

Once symbols have been created they are placed in the Library. Before looking at how to create symbols it will be useful to look at the function of the Library and how it deals with symbols. This is covered on the following pages.

The Library

The Library is the storage area where the content of a Flash movie is contained. All of the elements of a movie can be kept here and symbols are placed here automatically when they are created. They are then dragged from the Library onto the Stage to create instances.

Accessing the Library

1 If the Library is not already showing, select Window>Library from the Menu bar

2 Select an item and it will be displayed in the Preview window. The items in the Library are displayed here with an icon depicting their type

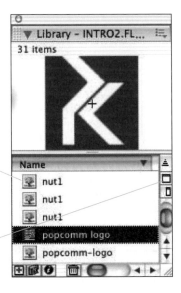

3 Click here to expand the Library window. This gives fuller details about each item stored in the Library

4 Click here to return to the standard Library window

When you first start creating a Flash movie you may think it is unnecessary to create numerous folders. However, the number of items you want to store in the Library will soon increase and folders are a good way to organise them.

If new folders are created in the main Library window these are known as root folders. These could be used for items entitled 'animations', 'buttons' and 'graphics'.
Folders can also be created inside other folders and these are known as sub-folders. These are created by double-clicking on an existing folder and creating a new folder as normal.

Creating new folders

One of the main functions of the Library is as a management system for all of the reusable items in a movie. In this respect it is similar to a file management system such as Windows Explorer in Windows or Finder on the Mac. As with these, it is possible to create folders and sub-folders for storing items. To create a folder:

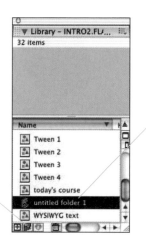

1 At the point where you want to insert a new folder click here

2 The folder name will be highlighted as 'untitled folder 1'. Type a new name for the folder

Deleting items

All objects within the Library can be deleted, including entire folders:

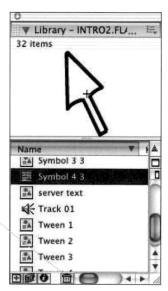

1 Select the item to be deleted and click here

2 A warning dialog box appears to check that you really want to delete this item. Click Delete

The Library menu

Some of the functions of the Library, such as creating new folders and deleting items, can be accessed from icons within the Library. Other functions are accessed from the Library Options menu:

Click here to sort items in the Library. This can be done by Name, Kind, Use Count (the number of times an item has been used in a movie), or Date Modified, depending on which heading is selected. Maximise the Library window to view all of the column headers.

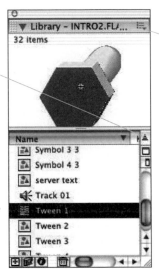

Click here to access the Library Options menu:

Some of the functions on the Library Options menu are:

- *New Symbol*. This creates a new symbol. (Symbol creation is covered on pages 82–85)

- *New Folder*. The same as using the new folder icon

- *New Font*. This allows you to import a new font style

- *New Video*. This allows you to import a video clip

- *Rename*. Enables the selected item to be renamed

- *Move to New Folder*. Creates a new folder and moves the selected item into it

- *Duplicate*. Makes a copy of the selected item

- *Delete*. The same as using the Delete icon

- *Edit.* Enables a symbol's properties to be edited

- *Edit with.* This enables you to edit bitmap images in an external image editing program, such as Fireworks

- *Properties.* Displays the selected item's properties i.e. its name and its behavior

If you have a Library collection from one movie and you want to use some of the items in another you can make them available.

Select File>Open as Library and the Open as Library dialog box will display all of the movies that have already been created. Select one then Open. This movie's Library will become available in the current movie and all of its contents can be used.

- *Linkage.* This is used to share elements of the current Library across numerous movies

- *Component Definition.* Defines the parameters for interactive components

- *Select Unused Items.* Selects all of the items that have not been used in the movie

- *Update.* This updates any editing changes that have been made to an imported item

- *Play.* This plays sounds, movie clips or buttons

- *Expand Folder.* By double-clicking, this expands the selected folder to view all of its contents

- *Collapse Folder.* This collapses the selected open folder so none of the items in it are visible

- *Expand All Folders.* This expands all of the folders in the Library

- *Collapse All Folders.* This collapses all of the folders in the Library

- *Shared Library Properties.* This displays the properties of any shared Libraries

- *Keep Use Counts Updated.* This automatically updates the counter for the number of times each item in the Library has been used

- *Update Use Counts Now.* This updates the use counter if Keep Use Counts Updated unchecked

Converting objects to symbols

Symbols can be created by two methods:

- Converting existing items into symbols

Frames are looked at in greater detail in Chapter Eight.

- Creating symbols from scratch (this is done in Symbol Editing Mode) and then adding content

All three types of symbols (graphics, buttons and movie clips) can be created using either method but the preferred option is different depending on the type of symbol being created:

- Since graphic symbols do not require any animation or interactivity they do not have to be edited beyond their initial state i.e. a single frame. Therefore they can be converted directly into symbols

Buttons and movie clips are created in Symbol Editing Mode. This has all of the same facilities as for creating items on the main Stage. Once the symbol editing process has been completed the item (along with its own timeline and frames) can be placed on the main Stage.

- Buttons and movie clips both require more than one frame's worth of content and so it is best to create a blank symbol and then add all of the content from scratch

Converting objects into symbols

1 Select the required objects on the main Stage. These can be stage level objects, overlay level object, text, groups or other symbols

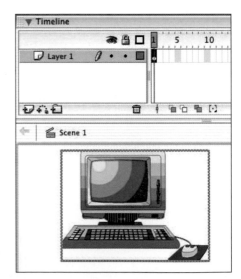

2 Select Insert>Convert to Symbol

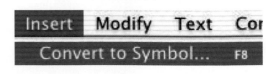

3 Type a name for the symbol. The default will be something like Symbol 7 (or the next sequential number for the symbols that have been created)

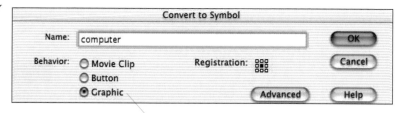

4 Select the type of symbol to be created (its behavior). Select OK

5 The symbol is placed in the Library and displayed in the Preview window

6 Click and drag the symbol to create an instance of it on the Stage

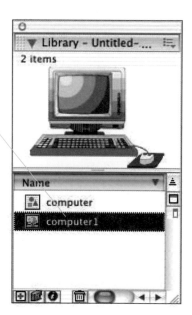

Creating a new symbol

For button or movie clip symbols it is best to create them from scratch using the New Symbol function. They can be created by converting an item into a symbol and then adding any additional elements that are required for the interactive button or the animation. However, since it can become slightly complicated as to what is a symbol and what is an item on the main Stage, it is probably best to stick to this method for buttons and movie clips:

Graphics can also be created from scratch using this method.

There are three ways to begin creating a new symbol from scratch:
Select Insert>New Symbol

or

Access the Library Options menu by clicking here and selecting New Symbol

or

Click the New Symbol icon in the Library

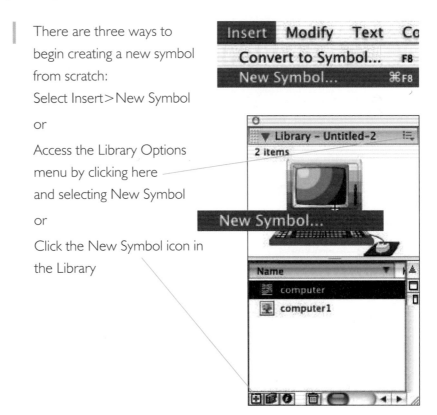

2 Each method accesses the

Create New Symbol dialog box. Enter a name and select a behavior for the symbol you want to create. Select OK

Creating button symbols involves creating four different states for the button:

- *one for before it has been activated (Up)*
- *one for when the mouse cursor passes over it (Over),*
- *one for when it is clicked on (Down), and;*
- *one for the area around the button that can activate its functions (Hit)*

Button symbols are looked at in more detail in Chapter Ten.

Movie clip symbols can be used independently on the main Stage. However, they can also be inserted into graphics, button symbols and even other animations. Movie clips are looked at in more detail in Chapter Nine.

3 Symbol Editing Mode is then accessed. This is the environment in which the symbol will be created. This is the Symbol Editing Mode for creating a button

This is the environment for creating a movie clip. It looks the same as the main Stage environment, but it is actually the movie clip symbol's own individual stage and timeline

4 The symbol is added to the Library as soon as it has been created, even if no content has been added at this point

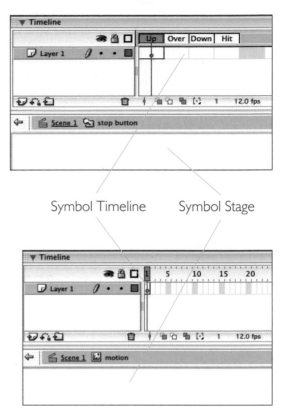

Symbol Timeline   Symbol Stage

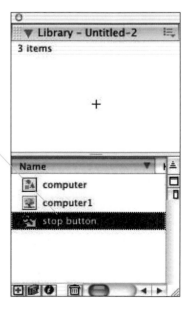

Symbol Editing Mode

Since new symbols are created with their own stage and timeline it can sometimes become confusing as to whether you are working on the main Stage or in Symbol Editing Mode. However, it is possible to identify in which mode you are working and switch between the two:

You have to double-click on the symbol icon in the Library and not the symbol name to access Symbol Editing Mode. If you double-click on the name this will just highlight it, so that its name can be changed by overtyping.

1 To open a symbol in Symbol Editing Mode, double-click on the symbol icon in the Library

2 Alternatively, click on the symbol icon at the right-hand side of the toolbar (to access a list of the symbols in the movie) and select one from the list

Scenes can be used to divide a movie up into manageable chunks, which is particularly useful if you are working with very large movies. Scenes are looked at in more detail in Chapter Nine.

3 The name of the active symbol is displayed here. This denotes you are working in Symbol Editing Mode

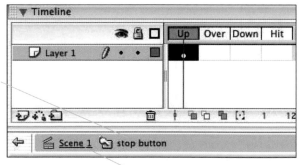

4 Click on the scene name to return to the main Stage

Editing symbols

Once a symbol has been created it can still be edited to change both its properties and its appearance. Its appearance can be altered by editing it in Symbol Editing Mode. In addition to the methods in Step 1 on the facing page, Symbol Editing Mode can also be accessed as follows:

Once changes have been applied to a symbol these will be applied to all instances of the symbol that have already been placed on the Stage. So if a circle symbol is changed to a square, all of the circle instances will become squares too.

- Select an instance of the symbol on the Stage. Select Edit>Edit Symbols from the Menu bar

- Select an instance of the symbol on the Stage. Select Edit>Edit Selected from the Menu bar

- Select a symbol in the Library. Select Edit from the Library Options menu (click on the small arrow next to Options to access the menu)

- Select a symbol in the Library and then double-click on the image in the Preview window

If you want to edit a symbol in its actual environment on the Stage, double-click on it on the Stage, or right-click (Windows) or Ctrl+click (Mac) on it and select Edit in Place. This allows you to edit the symbol while still viewing the relationship between it and the objects around it. The other objects are visible but greyed out while the editing takes place.

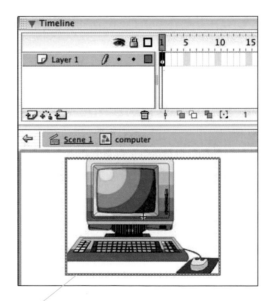

Once a symbol is in Editing Mode it can be modified in the same way as any other object. For example, this symbol could be rotated, resized or distorted using the Free Transform tool

Editing instances

It is possible to edit an instance's colour in a number of ways: changing its brightness, tint, and transparency. To edit an instance's colour:

1 Select an instance on the Stage by clicking on it once. Select the options from the Instance Properties Inspector

2 In the Instance Properties Inspector, click here to edit the brightness of the instance

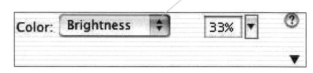

3 Enter values to edit the tint, i.e. create a new colour, or click here to select a colour

4 Click here to set the Alpha properties i.e. how opaque/transparent an object is

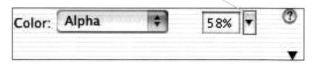

5 The Advanced settings enable you to select the colour properties and the alpha settings at the same time

Bitmaps, sound and video

In addition to creating drawing objects within Flash it is also possible to import bitmap images, such as photographs, and sound files. This chapter looks at how to import and edit both of these items and shows how they can be used to enhance a Flash movie. It also shows how to import video clips.

Covers

Using bitmaps | 90

Importing bitmaps | 91

Bitmap properties | 92

Bitmaps as fills | 93

Using sound | 95

Importing sounds | 96

Editing sounds | 97

Adding video | 99

Manipulating video | 100

Chapter Seven

Using bitmaps

Bitmaps are images that are created by using pixels (tiny coloured dots) to represent the image. Although Flash uses a different method to create graphics (vector-based, using a mathematical formula) it can support certain bitmap formats and it is possible to incorporate them into a movie.

Hard copy images such as graphics or photographs can be converted into bitmaps by using a scanner. This creates a digital image which can then be imported into Flash, providing it is created in an acceptable format.
Images taken with a digital camera can also be imported into a Flash movie.

Using bitmap images has a number of advantages:

- More complex images such as photographs can be used

- Bitmaps can be used as stand-alone images or they can be incorporated into backgrounds or fills

- There is greater opportunity for creating eye-catching content

The main drawback of bitmaps is that they generally take up more disk space than vector-based graphics, which adds to the size of a Flash movie and so has an adverse effect on the all-important downloading time. However, there are techniques that can be used to compress the size of bitmaps when they are incorporated in Flash movies.

Types of bitmaps

There are dozens of different formats for bitmap images. The ones that are supported by Flash are:

- BMP (Windows and Mac, with QuickTime)

It is also possible to import graphics from other vector-based programs such as Macromedia Freehand or Adobe Illustrator.

- PICT (Mac only)

- JPEG (Windows and Mac)

- GIF (Windows and Mac)

- PNG (Windows and Mac)

- WMF (Windows only)

Images in these formats can be imported into Flash and used in their original format. In addition to this, they can also be broken apart to allow for standard Flash image editing functions to be applied to them.

Importing bitmaps

Once a bitmap has been created it can be imported into a movie from your hard drive, from an external storage device such as a Zip drive, a CD-ROM or from a digital source such as a digital camera or a scanner. To import a bitmap:

1 Select File>Import from the Menu bar

If you want to import a bitmap directly from an external device, select the appropriate location at the top of the Import dialog box and then select the bitmap.

2 Locate the bitmap you want to import and select Open

When importing bitmaps, Flash will only display files whose format is supported by the program.

3 The bitmap is placed on the Stage and a copy is also placed in the Library. Although this is not strictly speaking a symbol, copies of the bitmap can be made by dragging it onto the Stage from the Library

Bitmap properties

When a bitmap is imported into a movie one of the most important issues is its file size. This is determined by the images resolution i.e. the number of pixels in the image. The higher the resolution then the larger the file size. This is measured in dots per inch (dpi) and if you are creating bitmaps for use in a Flash movie it is best to set the dpi to a maximum of 72. This is because computer monitors generally cannot display more than 72 dpi, so anything of a higher quality will be wasted and just lead to an unnecessarily large file size.

When a bitmap has been imported into a movie it is possible to edit some of its properties so that it appears at the highest quality but with the smallest file size. To edit a bitmap's properties:

1 Double-click on a bitmap in the Library (or click on it once and select Properties from the Library Options menu)

2 Edit the settings in the Bitmap Properties dialog box

Preview window

Allow smoothing – makes the image smoother

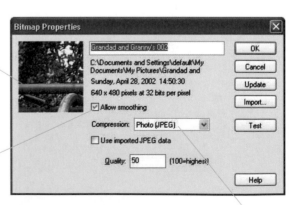

Compression options – determine how an image is compressed, thereby decreasing its file size

Bitmaps as fills

Once a bitmap has been imported into a movie it can be used as an individual image or it can be used as a fill for objects, in the same way as solid colours and gradients. To use a bitmap as a fill:

Once a bitmap has been broken apart, it becomes a stage level object and takes on the appropriate properties.

1 Select a bitmap on the Stage. Select Modify>Break Apart from the Menu bar

2 The bitmap becomes shaded, indicating that it has been broken apart

The Lasso tool and Magic Wand options can be used to select colours within a broken apart bitmap.

With the relevant tools selected, click on an area of colour on the bitmap. Depending on the Magic Wand options, an area of colour will be selected, which can then be used as a fill.

3 Draw an object on the Stage that is going to be filled with the bitmap

Once a bitmap fill has been chosen this becomes the default for all drawing objects, until another fill is selected.

4 Select the Dropper tool from the Tools panel

Tiling can produce some interesting effects for both drawing objects and backgrounds. Experiment with different images to see how they appear when tiled.

5 Click once with the Dropper on the broken apart bitmap

6 The tool turns into the Paint Bucket. Click inside the drawing object to add the bitmap fill

Make sure the bitmap-filled drawing object is deselected before you click on it with the Paint Bucket tool.

Using sound

Sound in Flash

In addition to its array of visual functions, Flash can also utilise sound files to give an extra dimension to a movie. These files have to be created outside Flash and then imported into a movie. They can then have some basic editing techniques applied to them. The three sound formats that can be used in Flash are:

- .WAV (Windows)

- .AIFF (Mac)

- MP3 (Windows and Mac)

There are two ways to use sounds in Flash:

- *An event-driven sound.* These are sounds that play when a certain action is performed, such as an interactive button being pressed. Event-driven sounds have to be downloaded completely before they play and the sound plays in its entirety before stopping, regardless of what else is happening in the movie

- *Streamed sounds.* These are sounds that are synchronised with the content of the movie, such as a soundtrack for a specific piece of animation. Streamed sounds are downloaded as each piece is required so even if it is a long sound file the user will be able to start listening to it before the whole clip has downloaded

 Flash MX supports MP3 sound files. MP3 has become one of the most popular file types for music on the Web and there are numerous sites where these can be downloaded. The most popular is www.mp3.com.

Creating sounds

Sounds can be created using a simple sound recorder such as the ones that come with most Windows operating systems (Sound Recorder) and the inbuilt one with Mac OS X. There are also numerous CD-ROMs that have sound collections on them, or you could try the following websites:

- http://www.webplaces.com/html/sounds.htm

- http://www.wavcentral.com/

Importing sounds

Sound files cannot be created directly within Flash so they have to be imported from the hard drive or an external storage source. To import a sound:

Once a sound has been imported and placed in the Library, it can be inserted into a movie by clicking and dragging it onto the Stage. The sound file will be placed on the selected layer at the nearest keyframe (see Chapter Eight for more information about frames and layers).

Select Control>Test Movie to hear the sound play or select the Play arrow in the Library Preview window.

1 Select File>Import from the Menu bar

2 Locate the required sound file and select Open

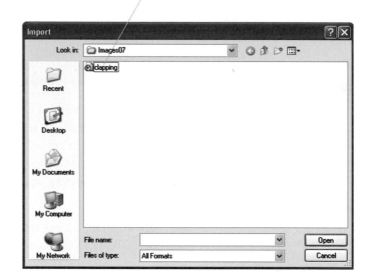

3 The sound is placed in the Library automatically. A digital representation of the sound is displayed in the Preview window

4 Click here to hear a selected sound

Editing sounds

Once sounds are in a movie, some simple editing techniques can be applied to them:

Changing the volume

1 Click the keyframe that contains the sound – it will be denoted by a straight line and its name displayed in the relevant Inspector

When working with sound files, create a new layer for each one. This will keep all of the sound files separate and make them easier to work with. For more information on layers, see Chapter Eight.

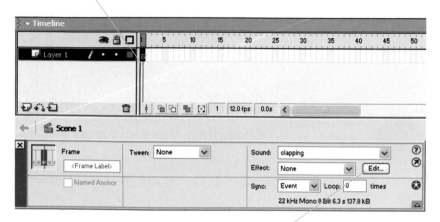

2 Click on the Edit button to display the sound file. The top window is for the left channel and the bottom window is for the right

When editing the volume of a sound, increase or decrease it by the same amount for each channel. Otherwise, when the sound is played there will be different sound levels for the left and right speakers.

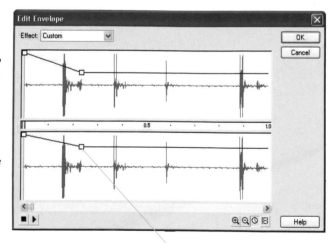

3 Click and drag the envelope handle to move the envelope line to increase or decrease the sound

Fading sounds in

Select a sound on the Stage and click on Edit in the Properties Inspector (step 2 page 97). Drag the envelope handle to the base of the window. Click the envelope line to add a new handle and drag this to the top of the window. This will cause the sound to fade in

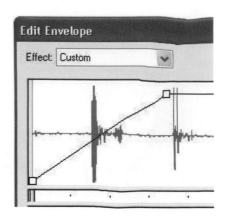

The time-in and time-out controls determine how much of a sound is cut off i.e. the whole of the sound is not played, just the portion between the two buttons.

Changing the start and end point

Drag here on the time-in button to make the sound begin at a different point. The same can also be done for the end point

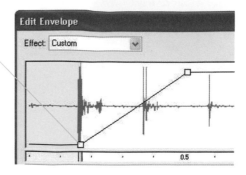

Click here to apply special effects:

Sound effects and properties

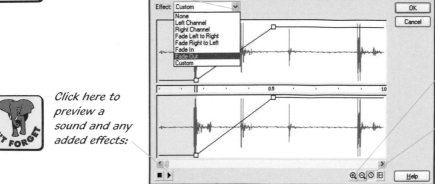

Click here to preview a sound and any added effects:

Zoom in or out here

Opt to view the sound timeline in frames or seconds

Adding video

A new feature in Flash MX is the ability to support video formats. This means that video clips can be inserted into movies and then played back over the Web or as stand-alone presentations. The following video formats can be used in a Flash movie, but only if Windows Media Player or QuickTime 4, or later, are installed to enable the playback of the video:

The best way to add your own video clips to a Flash movie is to capture them with a digital camcorder and then download them and edit them on your computer. This can be done with Windows Movie Maker (Windows) or iMovie (Mac).

- AVI (Audio Video Interleaved)

- MOV (QuickTime)

- DV (Digital Video)

- MPEG (Motion Picture Experts Group)

- WMV (Windows Media Video)

To use video in a Flash movie:

Select File>Import form the Menu bar and browse to a video file. Click on Open

If a video clip is inserted into a Flash movie, this will add considerably to the overall file size.

Enter the properties for the video and click OK

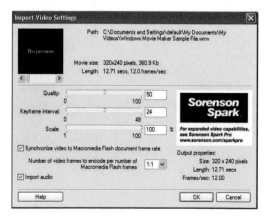

Manipulating video

Video files can be resized and rotated within a movie. However, they cannot have the distort or envelope functions applied to them. To manipulate a video clip:

1   Select the video clip and click on the Free Transform tool

Video clips can be converted into movie clip symbols in Flash so that they can be included within projects and also be reused without adding to the overall size of the published file.

2   Click on the Resize option and drag the resizing handles to edit the size at which the video is displayed

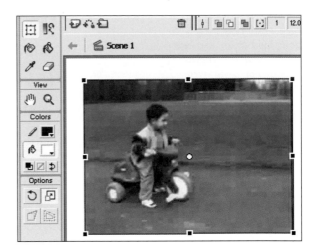

3   Click on the Rotate option and drag just outside a corner handle to rotate the video

If a video clip is made larger by resizing, the quality will deteriorate since it is not a vector object.

Frames and layers

Frames and layers are two important items for adding and controlling content in a movie. This chapter looks at inserting and editing frames and layers and how they can be used to simplify the editing process of a movie.

Covers

Working with frames | 102

Adding frames | 105

Deleting and copying frames | 107

Frame properties | 108

About layers | 109

Working with layers | 110

Inserting layers | 111

Deleting and copying layers | 112

Layer modes | 113

Layer properties | 114

Layers folders | 115

Mask layers | 116

Chapter Eight

Working with frames

Frames are the components of a movie that allow content to be added on the Stage. They also play a vital role in creating animations. There are different types of frames but they all serve the same basic purpose: to control the way content is displayed and viewed in Flash.

Keyframes

The most significant type of frame is a keyframe. This is like a master frame that denotes there has been a change in the content on the Stage. Every movie has a blank keyframe pre-inserted, but this is blank until content is added to the Stage, when a solid bullet point is displayed on the Timeline.

An empty keyframe, i.e. one with no content added on the Stage, is denoted by a blank frame

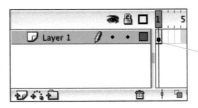

Once content has been added to the Stage, a solid circle appears in the keyframe

Frames can also have actions added to them (such as 'stop playing the movie' or 'move to a particular frame'). A keyframe that has had an action added to it is denoted with a small 'a' above the keyframe circle:

Actions can be added to keyframes to give them increased interactivity. See Chapter 10 for more on this

The terminology of frames and keyframes comes from the days when all animations were drawn by hand.

The keyframes were the ones where a specific event occurred in the animation, such as a character turning its head, and the regular frames were the ones where there was only static content. These frames were known as in-between frames i.e. the frames in-between where the actual animation took place. This is where Flash takes one of its main animation terms from – tweening. This is the technique for adding frames in between two keyframes in an animation.

(Tweening is looked at in Chapter Nine.)

Once content has been added to a keyframe, this will remain visible on the Stage until another keyframe occurs:

To move between keyframes and regular frames click and drag on the Playhead.

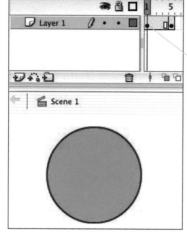

The content in the keyframe of frame 1 on the Timeline is a circle. Since another keyframe does not occur until frame 5, the circle will remain on the Stage until that point

If the content of a keyframe extends over more than one frame, this is known as a frame sequence. The end of this is denoted by a small rectangle on the timeline. This indicates that the content on the Stage will change after this.

The content in the keyframe of frame 5 on the Timeline is a square. At this point, the circle that appears in the first four frames will disappear and the square will replace it

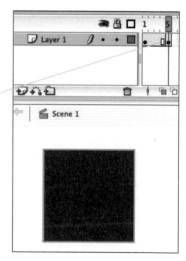

The speed at which frames are played in a movie (the frame rate) can be set by selecting Modify>Document from the Menu bar and then entering a value in the Frame Rate box in the Frame Properties dialog box. The default is 12 frames per second, which is considered best for display on the Web.

Some points to remember about keyframes:

- Keyframes have to be added if you want to create animations or include interactivity

- All movies have to have at least one keyframe

- All movies begin with a blank keyframe already inserted in frame 1 of the Timeline

If a new keyframe is inserted with no regular frames preceding it, these frames will be inserted automatically in the preceding frame sequence.

Regular frames

Regular frames contain the content of the nearest preceding keyframe and they can be used to determine the distance between keyframes and also the overall length of a movie. Regular frames are denoted by solid shading on the Timeline:

The end of a frame sequence is denoted by a hollow rectangle

Setting movie length with frames

A movie will not play beyond the last frame on the Timeline, whether it is a regular frame or a keyframe. In this way it is possible to set the length, in frames, of a movie. If you want a movie that is 20 frames long, then insert a regular frame or a keyframe at that point. (See the facing page for details on adding frames.)

Creating a background with frames

The background to a movie is a static element that can remain in place for the whole movie, allowing other objects to be placed on top of it.

When creating a background for a movie, place it on its own layer and position this layer at the bottom of any others in the movie. This will ensure that the background is always behind any other items on the Stage. For more on layers, see page 109 onwards.

| Create your background in the keyframe in frame 1

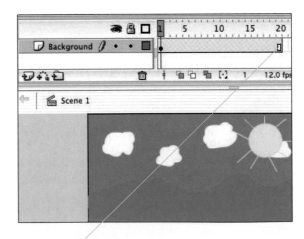

2 Insert a regular frame at the point where the movie will end. The background will occupy all of these frames

Adding frames

Regular frames and keyframes can be added at any point within a movie.

Adding regular frames

1 Select a blank frame on the Timeline where you want the new frame added

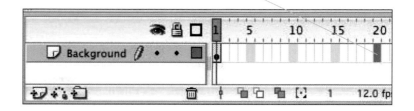

A regular frame can be added within a group of existing regular frames.
Drag the Playhead to the point where you want to add the frame, then do so as described on this page. This inserts a new regular frame to the right of the one that was selected. This can be done to extend the duration an item remains on the Stage during the movie. This increases the playing time of a movie.

2 Select Insert>Frame from the Menu bar, or right-click (Windows), Ctrl+click (Mac), and select Insert Frame

3 A regular frame is inserted and takes on the content of the nearest preceding keyframe

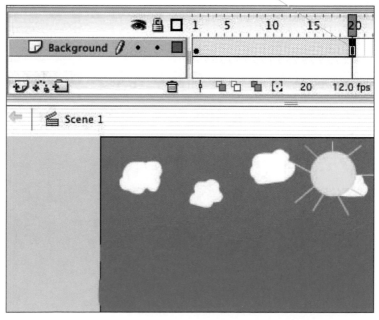

Adding keyframes

1 Select a frame on the Timeline where you want the new keyframe inserted

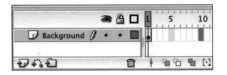

2 Select Insert>Keyframe (or Blank Keyframe) from the Menu bar, or right-click (Windows), Ctrl+click (Mac), and select Insert Keyframe (or Insert Blank Keyframe)

3 A new keyframe has the same content as the preceding keyframe. This can be edited accordingly for the new keyframe

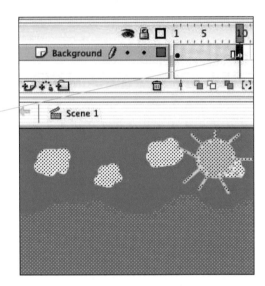

4 Except for the document background, a new blank keyframe has no content until items are added to the Stage in this keyframe

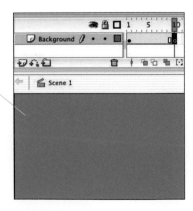

Deleting and copying frames

Deleting frames

Both regular frames and keyframes can be deleted from any point on the Timeline:

It is also possible to copy frames by selecting them and then dragging the selection to a new location. To do this, select the required frames by Alt+clicking (Windows) or Option+clicking (Mac) and then drag them to their new location. This will copy the frames and leave the original ones in place.

Select the regular frame or keyframe. Select Insert>Remove Frames or Insert>Clear Keyframe

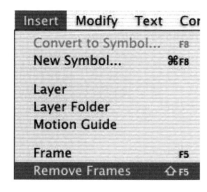

Copying frames

Frames can be moved from one layer to another by selecting them and then dragging them between layers. They can also be copied between layers by selecting them and dragging them as described in the HOT TIP above.

Select a single frame

by clicking on it on the Timeline, or select a range of frames by Shift+clicking on the first frame and then dragging over the range to be selected on the Timeline

2 Select Edit>Copy Frames from the Menu bar

When a range of regular frames is copied, the preceding keyframe is also inserted at the point where the frames are pasted on the Timeline.

3 Select the frame where you want the copied frames to be placed. Select Edit>Paste Frames from the Menu bar

Frame properties

Various properties can be assigned to frames. These include those for animation (Tweening) and interactivity (Actions), which are looked at in Chapters Nine and Ten respectively. Sound files that are located in a particular frame can also be edited in the Frame Properties Inspector. A fourth option is for adding labels and comments to a frame. A label is an identifier that is used to locate specific frames within a movie when working with interactive elements. Comments can be added as reminders about the content of a frame. They do not affect the published movie and are for information only in the editing environment. To add labels and comments:

Access the Frame Properties Inspector by clicking on a frame on the Timeline. Click here to add a label or a comment

Comments can be used as reminders to do certain things during the editing process. This could include a comment to add a particular item to a frame or to start an animation at a certain point.

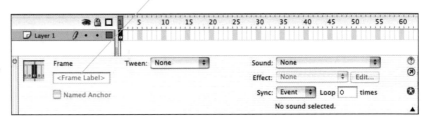

A label is denoted on the Timeline by a red flag and the name of the label

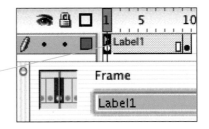

If the forward slashes are not inserted before the comment in the Frame Properties Inspector, then it will appear as a label on the Timeline.

A comment is denoted on the Timeline by two strokes and the name of the comment. These have to be inserted as forward slashes in the Frame Properties Inspector when the comment is being added

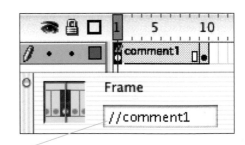

About layers

Layers are an organisation device in Flash that allows you to separate the content of a movie into manageable sizes. Layers act like sheets of glass placed one of top of another. Content can be added to each sheet and when they are compiled all of the content on the layers can be viewed together. Some points to remember about layers in Flash:

Use a new layer for each new element you add to the Stage.

It is possible to hide the content of layers. This is useful if you want to work on a layer without being distracted by the content on other layers. See page 113 for details about hiding layers.

It is possible to lock layers so that the content cannot change by accident.

- The order of layers is called the stacking order

- Content in the bottom layer that is covered by content on the next will not be visible, and so on through all the layers

- It is possible to change the stacking order of layers

- When creating a new item (such as a drawing object, an animation, a bitmap, a sound or an interactive button) it is a good idea to place it on a new layer. This will make it easier to edit and it means you will not have any other items getting in the way

- Only one layer can be selected and worked on at a time

- The background of a movie should always be on a separate layer, at the bottom of the stacking order

- Layers can be given their own individual names

- Dozens of layers can be added to a single movie

- When a movie is published, Flash displays the content in frame 1 of all of the layers used. It then displays the content in frame 2 of all of the layers and so on

- Layers can have their own stacking order if they contain stage level and overlay level objects. This internal stacking order is preserved if the layer is moved within the overall stacking order

- In Flash MX, layer folders can be added so that all of the content for a single element can be kept together within the same folder. Each layer folder can contain numerous different individual layers

Working with layers

The order in which objects appear in a movie can be changed by altering the position of its layers.

If no content overlaps on any layers then it may seem unnecessary to worry about the stacking order of them. However, if more content is added to any of the layers this could affect objects on other layers and the stacking order may have to be adjusted accordingly.

The layers of a movie display here

The top layer (triangle) is the one that appears as the foremost on the Stage. If it covers other objects, or parts of objects, behind it then these items will not appear. Similarly the second layer (the square) covers some of the object in the third layer

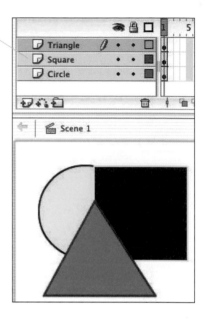

When moving a layer, a thick shaded line appears when you click and drag it. Place this above or below another layer to move it into this position.

Click and drag a layer to move its position in the stacking order. This changes the relationship between the objects on the Stage. In this case the Circle layer has been moved to the top, so the circle moves to the front on the Stage and covers the items behind it

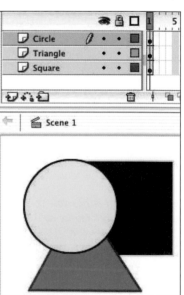

Inserting layers

All new movies are opened with one layer (entitled Layer 1), a Timeline and a blank keyframe in frame 1. Additional layers can be added at any time during the editing process and they also have a blank keyframe in frame 1. New layers can be inserted at any point in the stacking order of existing layers. To insert new layers:

1 Select the layer above which you want to insert the new layer

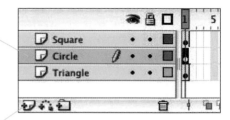

2 Click here to add a new layer or select Insert>Layer from the Menu bar

3 To rename the new layer, double-click on its name and overtype a new one

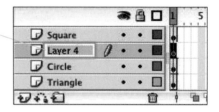

4 Enter content for the new layer. This will appear on the Stage according to the layer's position in the stacking order

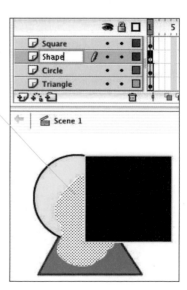

Deleting and copying layers

Deleting layers

If you decide you do not want to use the contents of a layer, it can be deleted from the movie:

If you delete a layer and its contents by mistake, select Edit>Undo from the Menu bar.

1 Select the layer to be deleted.

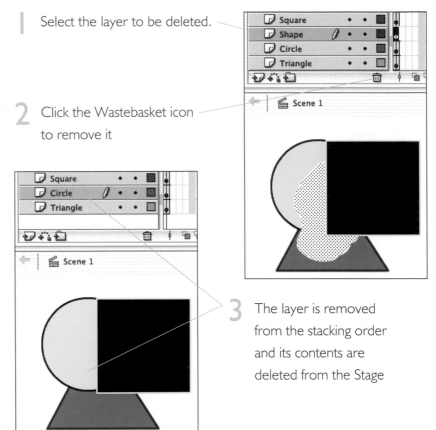

2 Click the Wastebasket icon to remove it

3 The layer is removed from the stacking order and its contents are deleted from the Stage

Copying layers

If you want to use the same, or similar, content from one layer, this can be copied and pasted into a new layer. This is done with the Copy Frames and Paste Frames commands as shown on page 107. To do this, insert a new layer in the stacking order. Then, select all of the frames in the layer to be copied and then copy and paste them into the new layer. The new layer retains its original name but it now contains content from the copied layer. All of the contents of a layer can be copied in this way, or only part of the contents.

Layer modes

Layers have four modes that can be selected, to make it easier when working with multiple layers:

Current Mode. This is the active layer on the Stage and is denoted by a pencil icon next to the layer name

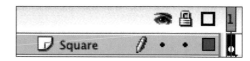

Hidden Mode. This hides the contents of the selected layer and is denoted by a red cross in the column below the eye

Locked Mode. This locks the contents of the selected layer so it cannot be edited and is denoted by a padlock in the column below the padlock icon

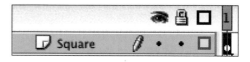

Outline Mode. This displays the contents of the selected layer as outlines only and is denoted by a coloured square in the column below the square

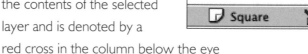

Individual layers can have Hidden, Locked or Outline modes applied to them. Also, all layers in a movie can have these modes applied by clicking on the icons at the top of the columns

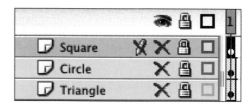

Layer properties

Various attributes within a layer can be determined in the Layer Properties dialog box:

The Layer Properties dialog box can also be accessed by right-clicking (Windows) – or Ctrl+clicking (Mac) – on a layer and selecting Properties from the contextual menu that appears.

| | Select a layer and select Modify>Layer from the Menu bar |

2   Select options for the layer's properties:

Click Show or Lock respectively to make the layer content visible or locked

Double-click here and overtype to change the layer name

In addition to normal layers there are also Guide and Mask layers. Guide layers are used to help control an animation's movement (see Chapter Nine). Mask layers are used to hide certain parts of other layers (see pages 116-118).

Select a layer type (see the HOT TIP)

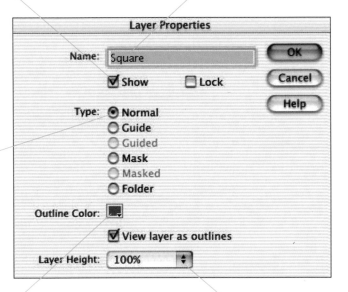

Click here to choose a colour if the layer is displayed in Outline mode

Click here to determine the height of the layer. The default is 100% but it can be changed to 200% or 300%, useful for viewing sound files in a layer

Layers folders

Groups of layers can be stored in individual folders, which makes it easier to keep track of the content of a movie. For instance, all of the layers that make up an animated logo sequence could be stored in a folder called Logo folder. This can help to organise the content of a movie in a neater and more organised fashion. To create layer folders:

Folders can be named in the same way as layers, by double-clicking on the folder name and then typing the new name.

Content cannot be placed within a folder itself, only the layers within it.

Click on the triangle next to the folder name to expand or collapse a folder.

1 Open a new movie and click here to add a folder for the existing layer

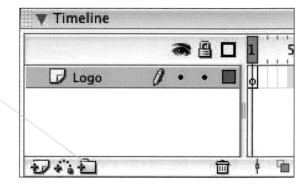

2 The layer is automatically placed within the folder. Click on the arrow next to the folder to display its contents

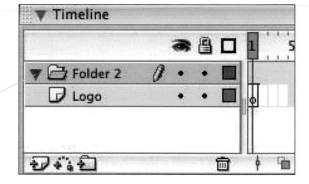

3 Add all of the content, on individual layers, into the folder for one specific topic

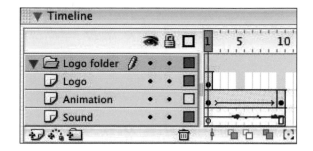

Mask layers

Mask layers are a special type of layer that works in a similar way to a stencil. A Mask layer can have objects added to it and it is then placed on top of another, regular layer. The content of the regular layer will only be visible through the content of the Mask layer: the rest of it masks the regular layer and hides any other objects. There are two important points to remember about Mask layers:

- Regular layers have to be linked to Mask layers for the mask to function

- The content of the regular layer will only be visible through the area on the Mask layer that has content. Although the mask content may look as though it is covering the regular layer, the reverse is true. The content on the Mask layer acts like a window, allowing the content behind it to be visible

Creating a Mask layer

Create a regular layer and add content

Once the concept of Mask layers is fully understood they can be used to create some highly artistic effects. It is an area that is worth persevering with and experimenting with.

When adding content to the layer that is going to be the Mask layer (in this case the layer in Step 2) it does not matter about its colour. This is because when it is acting as a mask the objects will be completely transparent to allow the content below it to show through.

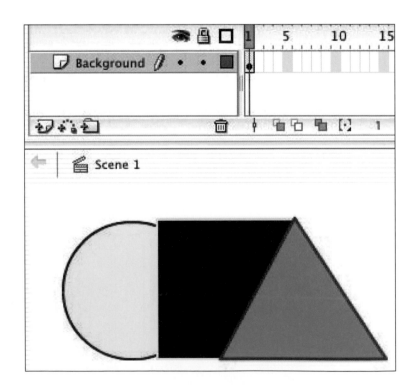

2 Add a new layer above the first and add content. Ensure it covers some of the first layer content

A Mask layer can be linked to several regular layers.

Mask layers are always above any regular layers which are linked to them. To link a regular layer to a Mask layer, click and drag the regular layer until the shaded line connected with the regular layer is directly below the Mask layer. Release and the regular layer becomes linked to the Mask layer.

To unlink a layer, click and drag it away from the Mask layer.

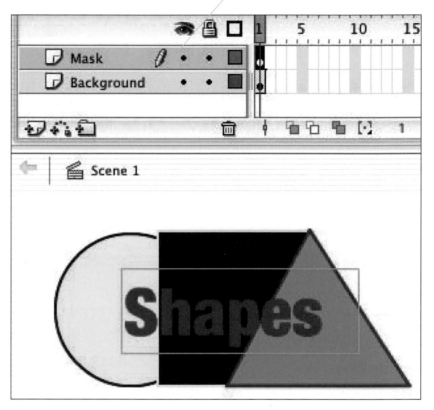

3 Select the layer that will be the Mask layer

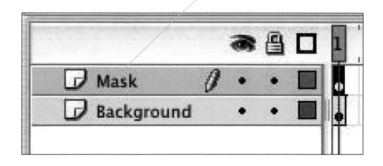

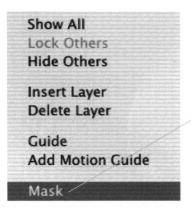

4 Right-click (Windows) or Ctrl+click (Mac) and select Mask

5 The Mask layer is now linked to the regular layer below. On the Stage the content on the regular layer is only visible through the content on the Mask layer

 A Mask layer is denoted by a green circle within a black square. A linked layer is denoted by a green square.

Animation

This chapter looks at the animation techniques that can be used in Flash. It shows frame-by-frame animation and also how to move objects using motion tweening and how to change one shape into another using shape tweening. It also looks at animating text and creating movie clips.

Covers

Animation basics | 120

Elements of animation | 121

Scenes | 124

Frame-by-frame animation | 126

Motion tweening | 129

Motion guides | 132

Motion guide orientation | 134

Shape tweening | 135

Animating text | 138

Distribute text to layers | 139

Movie clips | 141

Chapter Nine

Animation basics

Using layers for different parts of an animation can help reduce the overall downloading time of a movie. When Flash plays a movie it redraws the whole content of each layer that contains items that change. This includes static objects on the layer. If an element does not move it can reside on a separate layer and so will only have to be drawn once when it is downloaded.

Animation in Flash is, in many respects, just a technologically advanced version of traditional hand-drawn animation. In the days before computers, animations were created by drawing thousands of pictures and then playing them in sequence to create the animated effect. To reproduce the impression of movement, numerous drawings of an object were made, with each one slightly different from the preceding one. In this way the animators were able to create moving objects and characters using the same basic images.

In addition to creating moving objects, some items in an animation are static, such as the background. This difference helped form the hierarchy between the animation artists: the more highly paid and experienced ones created the moving items in an animation and the less well paid or less experienced artists usually stuck to the less technical drawings. This meant that there were groups of artists working on different layers within the same scene of animation. When all of the layers were collated, the final animation appeared.

In many respects Flash uses the same techniques as hand-drawn animations: objects can be animated on one layer, while other layers can contain elements that remain static throughout the movie. There are two types of animation that can be performed in Flash:

Although frame-by-frame animation can be time-consuming it can be better for complicated animations, such as showing someone talking.

- *Frame-by-frame animation.* This is a form of animation where an object's appearance or position is changed slightly from frame to frame to create the impression of movement. This involves using a new keyframe for each change and it can be a time-consuming process

- *Tweened animation.* This is where you select the starting and finishing points for an object and Flash animates it by filling in all the frames in between (hence the name). Motion tweening (moving objects) and shape tweening (changing the shape of objects) can both be applied

Elements of animation

The Timeline

The Timeline is the collection of layers/frames that contain the content of a movie. It can also be used to control how objects are animated. The default Timeline shows the layers, frames and keyframes. However, it can show the information in other formats:

1 Click here to change the way frames are displayed on the Timeline

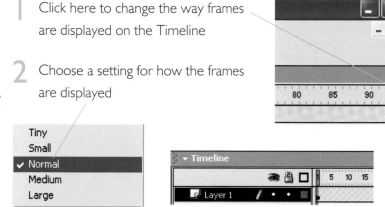

The Short option shrinks layers vertically. Use this if you want more layers to be visible at a time.

2 Choose a setting for how the frames are displayed

If Tinted Frames is checked on then all regular frames and keyframes will be tinted.

Tiny
Small
✓ Normal
Medium
Large

Short

✓ Tinted Frames

Preview
Preview In Context

Tiny

Large

Preview in Context shows the content for each frame but in the context of its actual size on the Stage.

3 Click Preview to see the objects in each frame on the Timeline

Timeline status bar

At the bottom of the Timeline is a status bar that contains important information about the movie:

| 21 | 12.0 fps | 1.7s |

Current frame being viewed

FPS during playback

Time elapsed to reach current frame (in seconds)

The Playhead

The Playhead can be used to move between frames to view their contents. When the Playhead is positioned over a frame, all of the content at that point is displayed:

If you click on a regular frame or a keyframe anywhere on the Timeline, the Playhead will move there automatically and display that frame's contents on the Stage.

Click and drag the Playhead to move through a movie. If this

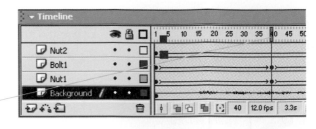

is done reasonably slowly it will display the results of any frame-by-frame animations, as the Playhead displays the contents of each frame

Onion skinning

When creating an animation it can be a great help to see what the objects in the preceding and succeeding frames look like. This way it is possible to make any subtle amendments to the item you are working on so it will fit in smoothly with those around it. This is known as 'onion skinning' and can be used as follows:

Create an animation. In this example it is a simple motion tween of a shape moving across the Stage

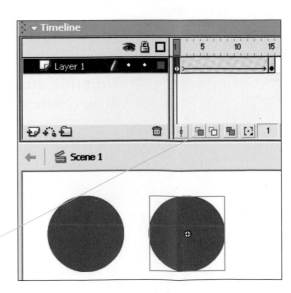

The button to the left of the Onion Skin button is the Center Frame button. By clicking on this you move back to where the Playhead is currently positioned. This can be useful if you have a movie with several hundred frames.

Select a frame in the animation. Click here to activate onion skinning

Content on locked or hidden layers is not affected by onion skinning.

3 The object in the selected frame and the two before and after it are displayed

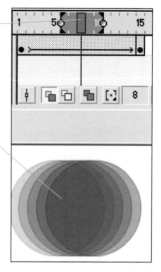

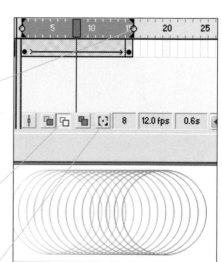

4 Click and drag here to extend the number of frames that are included in the onion skinning

The Always Show Markers option on the Modify Onion Markers menu determines that the onion skin markers are always visible on the Timeline even if onion skinning is not activated. Anchor Onion keeps the markers locked, rather than moving with the Playhead, as they do by default.

5 Click here to view the onion skinning in outline format

6 Click here to access the Modify Onion Markers menu. The bottom three options determine how many frames are affected by the onion skinning

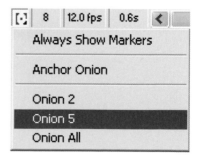

Scenes

Scenes in Flash are similar to their namesakes in a play: they are created separately but they are an important sequential part of the overall production. Scenes can be used to break up long movies into more manageable sizes, with different parts of the movie being broken up into separate scenes. For instance, if you have a movie that begins in an external location and then moves to an internal one, this could be broken up into two scenes. When using scenes it is worth remembering a couple of points:

- When creating a new scene, there is no evidence of other scenes in the editing environment, so if there are elements that are required throughout the whole movie, these will have to be recreated in the new scene

- Scenes play sequentially in the order they are created. However, it is possible to rename and reorder scenes in movies

Adding a new scene

New scenes can be inserted from the Menu bar or the Scene panel:

1   Select Insert>Scene from the Menu bar

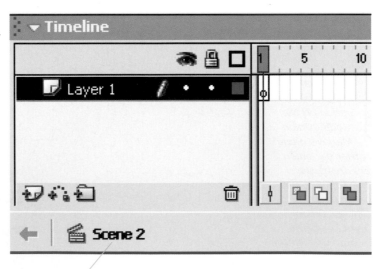

2   The name of the active scene is shown here

Alternatively:

Select Windows>Scene from the Menu bar to access the Scene panel

To delete a scene, select it in the Scene panel and click on the Wastebasket icon. This will remove the scene and all of its contents.

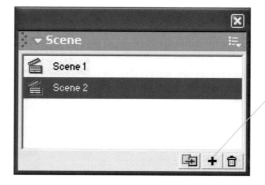

2 Click the Add button in the Scene panel to add a new scene

To reorder the sequence in which scenes play in a movie, click and drag on a scene in the Scene panel. Move it within the scene structure and then release. The movie will now play the scenes in this order.

Renaming a scene

Scenes can be given unique names, which makes it much easier when working with numerous scenes:

In the Scene panel, double-click on a scene

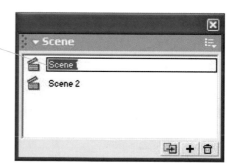

To move between scenes, access the Scene panel and select a scene. Also click on the Edit Scene icon at the right-hand side of the toolbar:

Click on the arrow to select a scene.

2 Type a new name for the scene in the Scene panel and press Enter or Return to apply the change

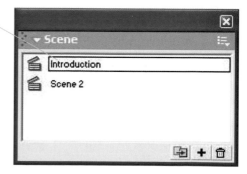

Frame-by-frame animation

A frame-by-frame animation involves inserting keyframes for each change in the animation and then editing the content accordingly. This way you are specifying the content for each frame of the animation: it is similar to drawing images on separate pages in a book and then flicking through it to create the animated effect. Frame-by-frame animations can be as simple or as complicated as you like, but the more complicated, then the longer it will take to edit the content for each frame.

Creating a simple frame-by-frame animation

To create an animation of an object moving across the screen:

Several different objects can be animated at the same point in a movie. Use layers for each individual element that is going to have animation applied to it.

Objects can be drawn in the Work Area rather than the Stage for the first keyframe of an animation. This will give the effect of the object 'flying in' from off the screen rather than starting on the Stage.

Once the background has been completed, lock it by selecting the background layer and then clicking on the column underneath the Padlock icon. This will ensure that you do not accidentally add any more content to the background layer.

1 Open a new movie by selecting File>New. Create a background on the existing layer. Insert a regular frame at frame 20

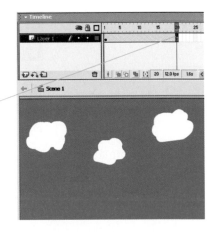

2 Insert a new layer above the background one and ensure the Playhead is at frame 1

3 At frame 1, add an object on the Stage

4 Select frame 5 then Insert> Keyframe from the Menu bar. The object will still be in the same position as it was in frame 1

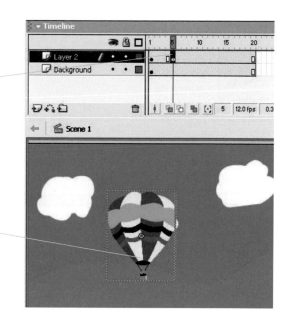

5 Click and drag the object and move it to a new position on the screen

6 Insert new keyframes at frames 10, 15 and 20 and reposition the object each time as in Step 5

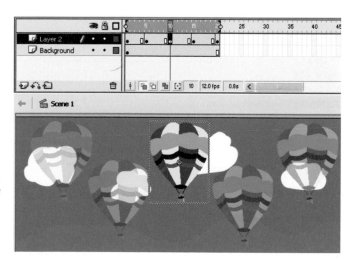

7 Select Control>Test Movie (or Test Scene) from the Menu bar to see the animation's progress. At this point it may look rather crude and jerky

To change the speed at which an animation plays (the Frames Per Second speed), select Modify>Document and change the value in the Frame Rate box (a higher value speeds up the animation and vice versa).

The Frame Rate box can also be accessed by double-clicking on the 'fps' (Frames Per Second) box on the Timeline:

12.0 fps

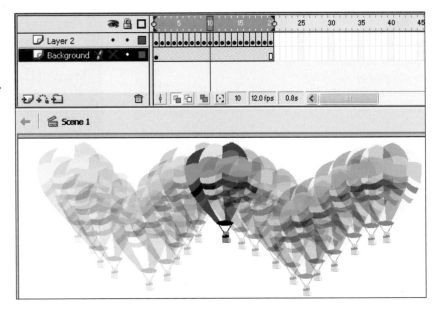

With this example the animation will keep playing indefinitely in its current state. In order to stop it once the object reaches the end of its path, a stop action has to be inserted at frame 20. This is looked at in Chapter Ten.

8 To smooth out the animation, select the frames between the keyframes that have already been inserted i.e. 2–4, 6–9 etc. Insert a keyframe into each one and reposition the object slightly each time. Click on the Onion Skinning button to see how the position of the object in each keyframe relates to those around it

9 When all of the keyframes have been added and the object repositioned, the path of the object can be seen by stretching the onion skinning markers across the length of all of the frames used. Select Control>Test Movie (or Test Scene) to see the animation in action

Motion tweening

Motion tweening is an animation technique that involves denoting the starting and ending point of an animation and then instructing Flash to fill in all of the frames in between. Only symbols, groups and text blocks can be used for motion tweens, but if a simple drawing object is required to be used in this way, Flash automatically converts it into a symbol. Motion tweens are excellent for depicting movement and a number of different properties can be defined, for additional creative power. To create a motion tween:

Motion tweening can create similar results to frame-by-frame animation, except it is usually quicker because Flash does a lot of the work for you. However, it does not allow for as much subtlety as a frame-by-frame effect.

Only symbols, groups or text blocks can be used in a motion tweening animation.

To insert a keyframe, select Insert>Keyframe from the Menu bar – alternatively, right-click (Windows) or Ctrl+click (Mac) – and select Insert Keyframe from the contextual menu.

Select File>New to open a new movie. In frame 1 add a drawing object. Convert it into either a graphic symbol or a group

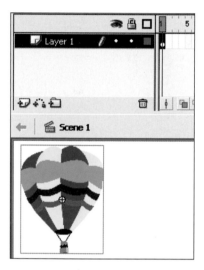

2 Move to frame 20 on the Timeline. Insert a new keyframe and reposition the object

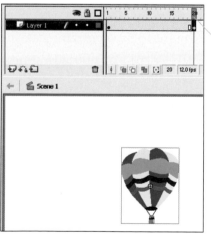

3 Select frame 1 again and then Insert>Create Motion Tween

If you use the Playhead to view an animation this will not be at the same speed as when viewed in the testing environment or when it is published.

Turn on onion skinning to see how Flash has inserted the in-between frames for the animation.

4 An arrow now spans the frames between the two keyframes.

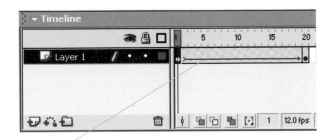

This denotes that a tween has been created

5 View the animation by clicking here on the Controller; dragging the

Playhead from frame 1 to frame 20; or selecting Control > Test Movie (or Test Scene) from the Menu bar

6 If there is a broken line in the Timeline between the two keyframes, this means that the tween has not been created successfully. This could be because the object was not converted into a symbol or a group (it has to be in the same state in both keyframes) or because a blank keyframe was inserted instead of a regular keyframe

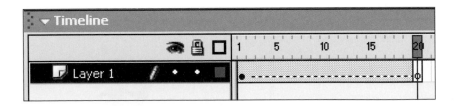

Editing a motion tween

Motion tweens can be edited so that the animation changes size, rotation and colour during the course of the tween. To apply editing techniques:

If these editing changes were applied to the motion tween in the example, it would begin small and transparent and then fade into view, increase in size and rotate 90 degrees. Effects like these can be used to give motion tweens a lot more versatility.

1 Select frame 1 and select the object with the Arrow tool. Select the Free Transform tool from the Tools panel. Resize the object by clicking and dragging one of the resizing handles

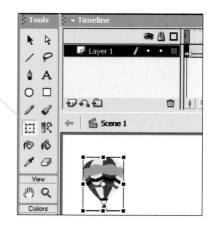

2 To ensure the object is completely transparent to start with and then fades in, in the Properties Inspector select the Alpha effect and set the value at 0%

Using the Alpha effect to make objects transparent is a popular technique for making graphics and text fade in and out of a movie.

3 Select frame 20. Select the object with the Arrow tool and then the Rotate option. Rotate the object by dragging just outside the rotation handles

Motion guides

In a basic motion tween, the object moves in a straight line between the starting and ending keyframes. In addition to this, it is also possible to create a freehand path for the object to follow as it moves between its starting and ending points. This is done with a device called a motion guide and it can be inserted as follows:

Motion Guide layers are always above any regular layers to which they are linked. A linked layer is recognisable on the Timeline because it is indented below the Guide layer.

1   Select the layer containing the motion tween

2   Click the Add Guide Layer button

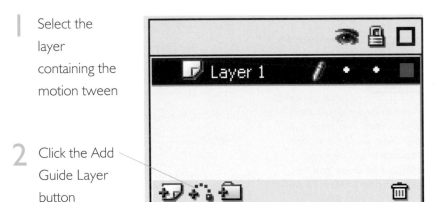

More than one layer can be linked to a Guide layer. Click and drag the required layer and place it below the motion guide. The object on this layer will follow the motion guide path.

3   The Guide layer is inserted above the layer containing the motion tween (now linked to the Motion Guide layer)

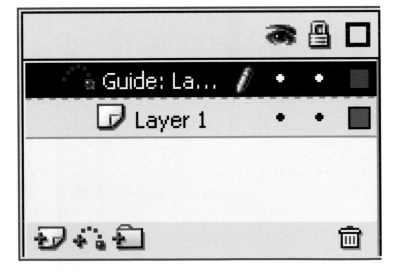

4 Select the Pencil tool in the Tools panel and the Smooth option

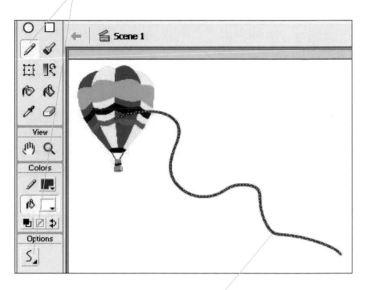

The path of a motion guide must start at the centrepoint of the object in the first frame and finish at the centrepoint of the object in the last frame. Otherwise the object will tween directly between the two points.

5 Draw a freehand line joining the start and end points of the object

6 The motion tween will follow the path of the line

For each new motion guide path you want to create, a new Motion Guide layer has to be inserted.

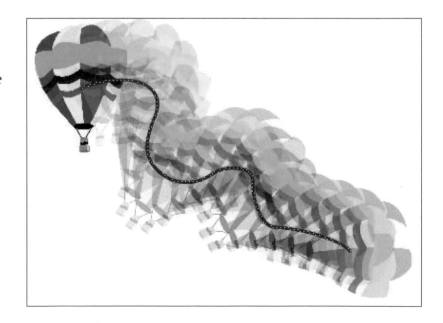

Motion guide orientation

It is possible to alter the way a motion tween moves along the motion guide path. This can have a significant effect, depending on the type of object being tweened.

The Easing slider can be used to change the speed at which a motion guided animation performs.

Drag the slider down to make the animation start slowly and speed up. Drag the slider up to make the animation start quickly and slow down at the end.

If the Snap box is checked on, an object's centre point will snap to the motion path even if it is moved within its frame. If you want to move an object's centre point away from the motion path, check this box off.

1 Click on the first frame of the linked layer (not the Guide layer) to access the Frame Properties Inspector

2 The type of tween should be displayed here. Enter a value for Ease to determine how quickly or slowly you want the tween to begin.

Check on the Orient to path box. This ensures the centre point of the object is rotated around the guide path

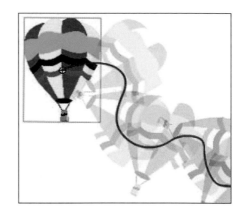

3 Alternatively, check off the Orient to path box to keep the object parallel as it follows the guide path

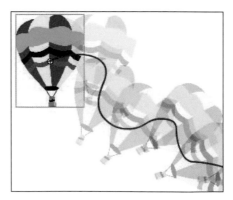

Shape tweening

The third type of animation that can be performed in Flash is shape tweening, or morphing. This is where one shape changes into another during the course of the animation e.g. turning a letter A into a number 2. This type of animation can only be done with simple shapes, broken apart text and stage level objects. Shape tweening cannot be applied to symbols, groups or bitmaps. To create a shape tween:

 Shape tweening is an effective technique but it should not be overused in a movie, or else the impact will be diminished.

1 Select File>New to open a new movie. In frame 1 select the Text tool. In the Text tool Properties Inspector type the letter A in a large font size (72 points or above)

2 Select the A on the Stage and select Modify>Break Apart from the Menu bar. This will enable shape tweening

 A blank keyframe is inserted in frame 20 at Step 3 because the content is completely different from the previous keyframe. If the content was the same but was going to appear in a different position (as in a motion tween) then a regular keyframe would have been inserted rather than a blank one.

3 Select frame 20 and insert a blank keyframe (Insert> Blank Keyframe). With the Text tool, type the number 2, the same size as the A in frame 1. Break it apart as above

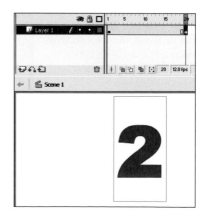

If you are using text for shape tweening and the tween does not work properly, make sure that both pieces of text are broken apart.

The Distributive and Angular options in the Property Inspector determine how the tween operates. The Distributive option is better for curved objects; Angular is better for objects with straighter lines and corners.

It is possible to tween more than one letter or number together, but the results are erratic. If you want to shape tween a whole word, do it by putting each letter on a separate layer and creating each tween individually.

4 Select frame 1 to access the Frame Properties Inspector. Select the Tweening tab and opt for Shape as the type of tweening

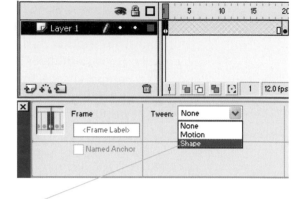

5 Turn on onion skinning to see the path of the shape tween

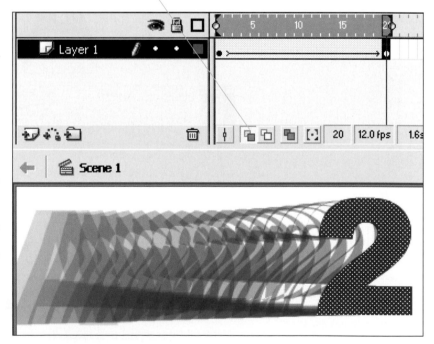

6 It is possible to change the size, colour and orientation of the tweened objects, in their keyframes, by using the drawing tools and their options. This can give added effect

Shape hints

Sometimes the results of a shape tween can be less than ideal; during the course of the tween the object looks more like an ungainly blob rather than one item morphing into another. To improve the tweening process, it is possible to add shape hints to each object. These are corresponding points on each object that act as guides for the tween to follow. To add shape hints to a shape tween:

Up to 26 shape hints can be added to the objects in a shape tween. These are labelled a–z.

1. Select the object in frame 1. Select Modify>Shape>Add Shape Hint from the Menu bar

2. Position the shape hint on the object in frame 1

Each object in the shape tween has to have the same shape hint applied to it, i.e. if the first object has an 'a' shape hint then the second object has to have the same one.

3. Move to the object in frame 20 and position the shape hint in the same corresponding position as for the object in frame 1

4. Continue until a suitable number of shape hints have been added to each object

Animating text

One of the most common uses for Flash on the Web is creating animated text. This is where text moves across the screen from left to right, or vice versa, or fades in and out from a particular point. In some cases, numerous pieces of text are animated within a single movie and, if it is done well, this can create a visually striking effect. To create animated text:

Text blocks have to be converted into graphic symbols for them to be animated properly. Create the text block and select Insert>Convert to Symbol and select Graphic as the behavior from the Create New Symbol dialog box.

1 Create a text block and convert it into a graphic symbol. Create a motion tween to move it across the screen

2 Select the text on the Stage in frame 1. In the Frame Properties Inspector set the Alpha option to 0%. This will make the text fade in as it progresses through the tween

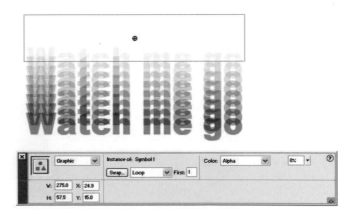

To create fading text at the same point on the Stage, create a motion tween maintaining the same position for the text in both keyframes. Then apply Alpha settings to the text at one of the keyframes.

3 Create tweens with text on several layers for added effect. Vary the start and end points of the tweens to achieve variety

Distribute text to layers

In Flash MX, the use of animated text has been simplified by enabling text blocks to be broken apart and the individual letters placed on separate layers. This is an invaluable function if you want to animate individual letters of a text block rather than the whole block. To do this:

If the text block is not broken apart before it is distributed to layers, then the whole block will just be placed on a new layer.

1 Create a text block and select Modify>Break Apart from the Menu bar

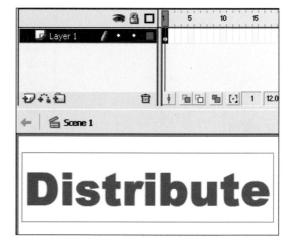

Individual letters can also be manually distributed to layers once a text block has been broken apart.

2 Select Modify>Distribute to Layers from the Menu bar. This will automatically place each letter on its own layer

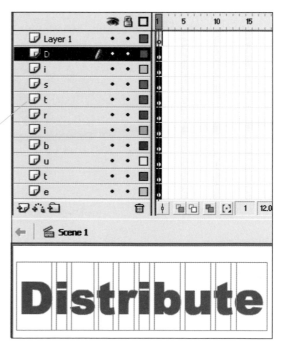

3 Animate each individual letter by creating a motion tween with each one. This creates the effect of all of the letters moving independently of the others

Animating text on different layers can produce very dramatic effects. However, do not overuse this feature as it can become rather distracting to see too much text moving around in a Flash movie.

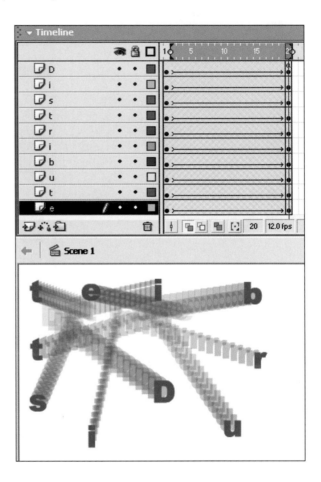

4 Select Control>Test Movie (or Control>Test Scene) to view the animated text effect

Movie clips

Movie clips are symbols that act like self contained animations: they have their own Timeline and once they are created they are placed in the Library. They can then be reused by inserting them anywhere on the main Timeline. This is useful if you have an animation that you want to use several times. To create a movie clip symbol:

Any elements that can be added to an animation in the main editing environment can also be added to a movie clip symbol.

1 Select Insert>New Symbol from the Menu bar. Name the symbol and select Movie Clip

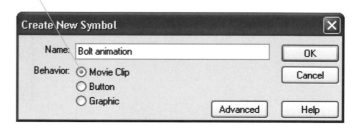

No matter how long a movie clip symbol is (and they can extend over dozens of frames) they are always placed in one frame on the main Timeline.

2 Movie Clip Editing Mode looks the same as the main Editing Mode except that the movie clip icon is shown here. Create the animation as you would for one on the main Stage

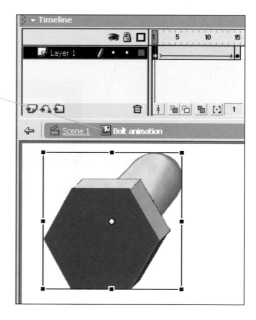

3 When the movie clip is completed, click on the scene number to return to the main Editing Mode. The movie clip symbol will be placed in the Library and can be reused throughout the movie

Movie clips can be added to interactive buttons (see Chapter Ten).

4 The movie clip is added to the Library and can be previewed by selecting it and then clicking here in the Preview window

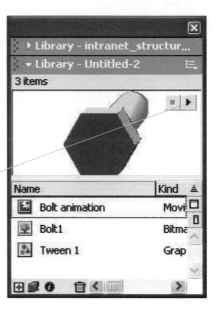

5 Create instances of the movie clip by dragging it onto the Stage from the Library. The instances can then be resized or rotated by using the Free Transform tool

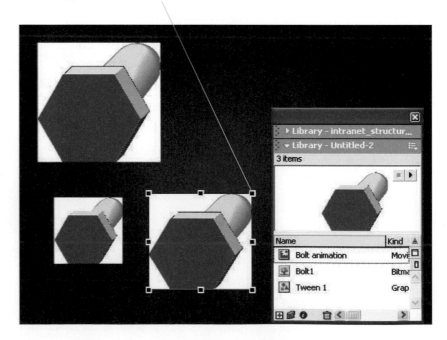

Interactivity

Giving the user the power to interact with a movie is an important part of Flash. This chapter looks at the ways in which this interactivity can be achieved with frames and buttons and also looks at some options for using interactive actions. This includes creating features such as disjoint rollovers and rollover navigation bars, which can be used to great effect on Web pages or in presentations.

Covers

Types of interactivity | 144

Frame actions | 145

Adding Stop and Play actions | 148

Adding Go To actions | 149

Inserting a preloader | 151

Button symbols | 153

Adding actions to buttons | 156

Adding movie clips and sounds | 158

Creating disjoint rollovers | 159

Adding invisible buttons | 160

Creating rollover navigation bars | 161

ActionScript | 164

UI Components | 166

Named anchors | 168

Movie Explorer | 170

Chapter Ten

Types of interactivity

In addition to its graphical and animated elements, another important aspect of Flash is its interactive functions. These can allow the movie author to instruct the program to perform certain actions when it reaches a certain frame, or an action can be performed when the user clicks on a particular button. Also, interactivity can be achieved with text fields, where an action is performed as a result of the user entering text in an editable text box.

For interactivity to occur in a movie there need to be certain elements present:

- An event, which is something that sets the action in progress. This can be a movie reaching a particular frame or the user clicking a button

- An action, which is performed when the event occurs

- A target, which is the item upon which the action is performed

Actions can be inserted into frames or button symbols. If it is a frame action it can be inserted in the layer where the interactivity is to take place, or it can be placed on a separate layer. In a button symbol the action can be placed in one of the states of the button i.e. when the cursor is moved over it, when it is clicked on or when the mouse button is released.

If an action is inserted on a separate layer, the action will apply to all of the frames at that point in the movie, regardless of how many layers there are.

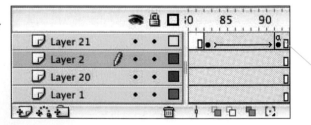

A frame with an action inserted. This is denoted by the small 'a'

Creating interactivity with actions can be a complex business, using some elements of computer programming, the finer points of which could take up a whole book themselves. This chapter gives an overview of interactivity and shows some of the commands that can be used.

Frame actions

Frame actions are placed in a frame and when the Timeline reaches this frame the action passes on an instruction. This could be to stop a movie playing at that point, turn off any sound that is playing or jump to another frame within the movie.

Adding frame actions

Actions can only be inserted into keyframes. If they are inserted into regular frames, they will be placed in the nearest preceding keyframe.

1 Click once on the frame where you want to add the action. Select Window>Actions to access the Frame Actions panel

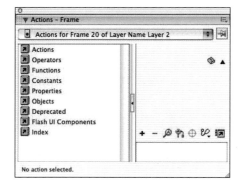

2 Click once on the Actions button to access basic actions. Double-click on one to add it to the movie. It will then appear in the Actions panel

Numerous different actions can be added to the same frame. When multiple actions are included, they occur in the order in which they were placed.

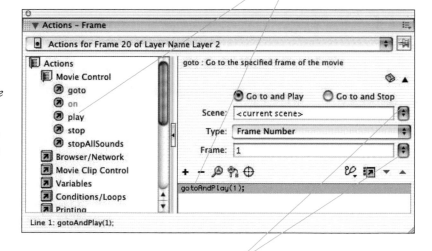

3 Click the arrows to view and specify the parameters for the selected action

Types of basic actions

The basic actions that can be inserted into a frame are:

- *Go To.* This instructs the movie to jump to the specified frame

- *Play.* This instructs the movie to begin playing

- *Stop.* This stops the movie playing at the specified point. It can be restarted using the Play action

- *Toggle High Quality.* This displays graphics at a higher or lower quality. Also referred to as anti-aliasing

- *Stop All Sounds.* This turns off any sounds that are playing at this point in the movie

- *Get URL.* This instructs the movie to open the specified URL i.e. Web page

- *FS Command.* This lets the movie communicate with the program that is hosting it i.e. a Web browser

- *Load/Unload Movie.* This loads, or unloads, the movie into a Web page

- *Tell Target.* This can be used to interact with other Flash movies by using actions within the current one

- *If Frame is Loaded.* This instructs the movie to perform an action if a certain frame has already been downloaded

- *OnMouseEvent.* This defines a mouse event that has to take place for an action to occur. This is used mainly with object actions, such as for buttons and movie clips

Some of the above frame actions (such as Stop, Play, Toggle High Quality, Stop All Sounds and Go To) are reasonably straightforward. Others (such as FS Command, Set Property and Set Variables) require a certain amount of programming knowledge.

More actions

The other categories of actions are:

- Operators

- Functions

- Constants

- Properties

- Objects

- Deprecated (contains ActionScripts that have been replaced by new elements in Flash MX to meet accepted ActionScript standards). Deprecated elements are still supported

- UI Components

Click once on a category to see the various actions that are available.

Deleting actions

Any action can be deleted from within the Actions dialog box:

When an action is deleted there is no warning box asking if you are sure you want to delete the action. This may not be a problem if it is a simple action such as a 'Stop' one. However, if it is a more complicated action, with several parameters, it could take longer to regenerate it. Make sure you really want to delete an action before you do so.

Click here to change the order in which actions appear

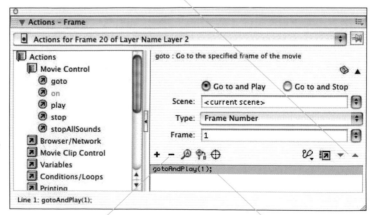

2 Click here to delete the action

1 Access the Frame Actions panel and select an action in the Actions panel

Adding Stop and Play actions

Two of the most commonly used actions are Stop and Play. These do exactly as they say and they can be used at the beginning of a movie or at any point throughout it. The Stop action halts the whole movie at the point where the action is inserted. To restart the movie a Play action has to be activated after the Stop action. Stop actions can be used to stop an animation playing continuously. To add Stop and Play actions:

By default, a Flash movie on the Web plays automatically once it is loaded. If you want to pause it at the start, add a Stop action in frame 1 of the movie. This could be used if you want the movie to begin only after the user has performed an action, such as clicking on a button.

If a movie is being used as a stand-alone application, the default is to pause it. To make it play automatically, a Play action (or a Go To and Play action) would have to be inserted in frame 1.

1 Select the frame where you want the movie to stop

2 Access the Frame Actions panel by selecting Window>Actions from the Menu bar

3 Double-click on the Stop action to place it in the Actions Panel

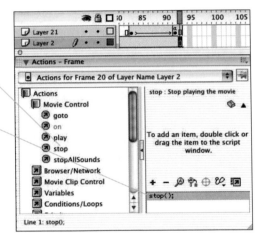

Actions can also be added to the Actions panel by dragging and dropping them from the Toolbox list (left panel).

4 Add any other actions you want to include after the Stop action and add Play to restart the movie

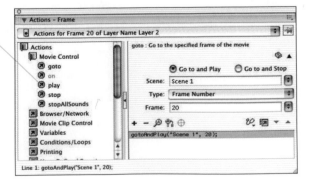

Adding Go To actions

Unless instructed otherwise, a movie will play all its frames in order. However, by using actions you can change the sequence they play in. You could do this if your movie is an interactive game. In one frame could be a question, and the movie would then move to different frames depending on the answer. To do this you have to insert values for each Go To action. To insert a Go To action:

1 Select a frame where you want a Go To action and access the Frame Actions panel as shown on the facing page. Double-click on the Go To action

The Go To action can be used to jump to any frame in any scene in the movie.

2 The Go To action is added to the Actions dialog box. By default it goes to the first frame of the current scene. This can be changed

Labels can be used to identify frames as the destination for a Go To action, rather than just the frame number.

3 Click the arrow next to Scene and choose a different scene from the drop-down list

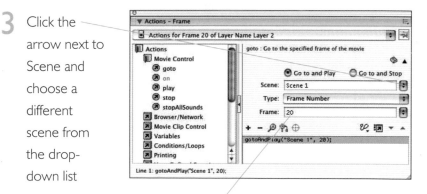

4 Enter a different frame number by adding a value here

If the target frame for a Go To action is the previous one then there is a danger of inserting an unwanted loop in the movie. If the movie goes back to the previous frame, plays its content and then moves onto the next frame, the Go To action will send it back again, and so on. Another action would have to be inserted in the target frame to avoid it going straight to the next sequential frame (unless a loop effect was intended).

5 Select a target frame for the Go To action by clicking on Type and selecting an option. This can be a frame number, a label,

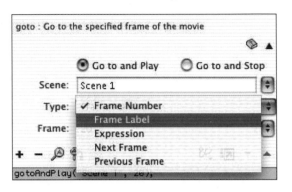

an expression (a formula based on variable information) or the next or previous frame

6 By default, the Go To action also inserts a Play action. If you want the movie to stop when it reaches the target frame check off the Go to and Play box

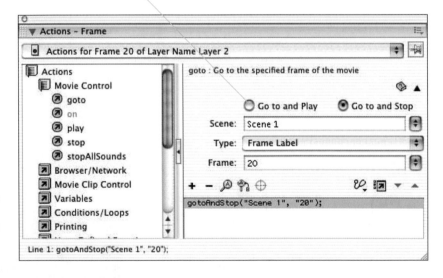

By default, the Enable Simple Frame Actions option is checked off. This is because it can be irritating for the frame actions to be active when you are editing a movie.

7 Select Control>Enable Simple Frame Actions from the Menu bar to allow you to see how frame actions operate, while you are still in Editing Mode

Inserting a preloader

To rename a scene, select Modify>Scene and type in the scene name in the Scene dialog box.

If you have created a long movie, it may take a few seconds for it to download and start playing. This could lead to the user concluding that, since nothing is happening, they should move on somewhere else. To overcome this problem it is possible to create a preloader. This is a message or small animation that assures the user that the movie is loading and will appear shortly. To create a preloader:

Make sure the preloader scene comes before the main movie one.

1 Create a new movie by selecting File>New from the Menu bar. Create a minimum

of two scenes, one for the preloader and one for the main part of the movie. Name Scene 2 Main Movie and create your movie. Name Scene 1 Preloader and enter suitable content on the Stage

Since Flash movies use streaming, only part of a movie has to be downloaded before it starts playing. Therefore, when specifying a frame that has to be loaded it does not have to be the last one in the movie. It just has to be enough of the movie to allow it to play while the rest is downloading.

2 Insert a new layer and call this Preload Actions. Select frame 1. In the Frame Actions panel, select If Frame is Loaded and specify a frame in the Main Movie scene. This specifies the target frame that has to be loaded before the next action takes effect

To make sure you specify the correct frame for If Frame is Loaded, check in the Testing environment to see how many frames it takes to preload the main movie. Enter this as the target frame in Step 2 here. For more on testing movies see Chapter Eleven.

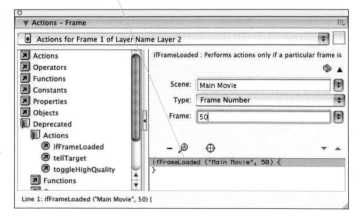

The preloader will keep playing until the criteria in the If Frame Is Loaded action are met. If this takes a reasonable amount of time (over 30 seconds) then it is worth creating a preloader scene that can hold the user's attention.

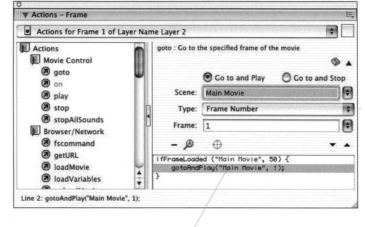

3 Enter a Go To and Play action underneath the If Frame Is Loaded action. This is the action that will be performed if the criteria for the first action are met i.e. frame 1 of Main Movie will start playing if frame 50 has already been loaded. If it is not met it will move to the next frame

If a movie is short or small in file size, the preloader may be redundant because the target frame for loading will be in place even before the preloader can be displayed.

4 Insert a keyframe in frame 2 of the preloader scene and select it. In the Frame Actions panel, enter a Go

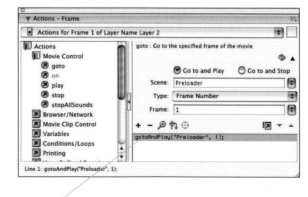

To and Play action and set the parameters as current scene, frame 1. This will send the Timeline back to frame 1 of the preloader scene. It will then check the actions here. If the criteria have not been met it will go to frame 2 again and so on. Once the criteria in frame 1 are met the Timeline will go to the Main Movie scene and begin playing at the specified frame

When adding the Go To action, make sure the Go to and Play box is checked on.

Button symbols

Creating button symbols

As well as inserting actions into frames in a movie, interactive actions can also be used in buttons. These are symbols that react in certain ways when they are clicked by the user or even when the mouse cursor passes over them. Button symbols can be used in the same way as other symbols: they are created in Symbol Editing Mode which then places them in the Library. They can then be dragged onto the Stage, where they become instances of the original button symbol. When a button is created it has four elements, or states:

Using different coloured gradient fills for each state of a button symbol can produce a satisfying effect, where the button appears to glow.

- *Up.* This is how the button appears initially on the Stage, before it has been accessed

- *Over.* This is how the button appears when the mouse cursor is passed over it

- *Down.* This is how the button appears when it is clicked on by the user

- *Hit.* This is the area around the button that is active i.e. if it is clicked it activates the appropriate state. The hit state is invisible in the published movie

To create a button symbol:

Button symbols always have four frames and they act like mini movie clips.

1 Select Insert>New Symbol from the Menu bar

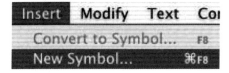

2 Name the button and select Button as its behavior. Click OK

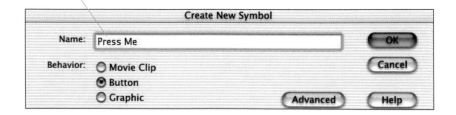

...cont'd

It is possible to tell when you are in button Symbol Editing Mode because the button symbol and its name are highlighted below the Timeline, next to the scene name. Also, the four frames have the names of the corresponding button states above them i.e. Up, Over, Down and Hit.

3 Symbol Editing Mode for a button symbol is activated. This contains four frames, with a keyframe pre-inserted in the first one. The crosshair on the Stage denotes the centre of the button. Create a button around the crosshair

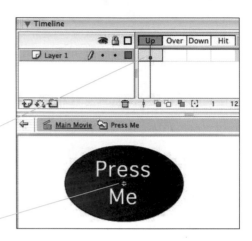

Insert a blank keyframe by selecting Insert>Blank Keyframe from the Menu bar.

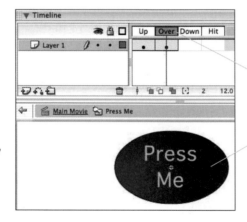

4 Select the Over frame and insert a keyframe. Change the formatting of the button

If you only want to make small changes to an object in a preceding keyframe, such as changing the colour, use the Insert>Keyframe command.

5 Select the Down frame and insert a keyframe. Change the formatting of the button again, if required

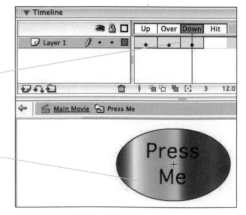

You can make the area defined for the Hit state any colour you like, since it does not appear in the published movie. However, it is a good idea to make it a different colour from the first three states of the button. This way you will know what is the Hit state when you are in Symbol Editing Mode.

6 Select the Hit frame and insert a blank keyframe. Draw an object around the crosshair that is large enough to cover the biggest object in the button. This is the area that will activate the button

7 Click on the scene name to return to the main Editing Mode. The button symbol will have been placed in the Library. Select the button and click and drag to create an instance on the Stage

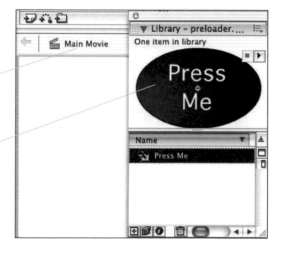

If the Library is not visible, select Window> Library from the Menu bar.

If you try to edit a button instance while Enable Simple Buttons is active, you will only see the different states of the button. Deselect this to perform editing tasks on the Stage.

8 Select Control>Enable Simple Buttons from the Menu bar. This enables you to see how the button performs in its different states, without having to leave the main Editing Mode. The button can also be tested by selecting Control>Test Movie (or Test Scene)

Adding actions to buttons

The same actions that are used for frames can also be used for objects such as buttons and movie clips. However, they are triggered in slightly different ways: button actions are triggered by mouse events (i.e. an action performed by the mouse) and movie clips are triggered by clip events, which can either be actions by the mouse or a function performed by the movie clip itself. For both types of object the actions that can be added are the same. To add an action to a button:

Button actions should be added to the instance on the Stage rather than the symbol in the Library.

Button actions can be added to the button without first selecting an OnMouseEvent.

Place an instance of a button on the Stage and select it. Access the Button Actions panel by selecting Window>Actions from the Menu bar

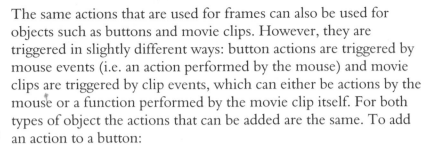

2 Select Actions>Movie Control, and select On by double-clicking on it

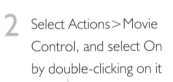

3 Select a mouse event that will activate the action

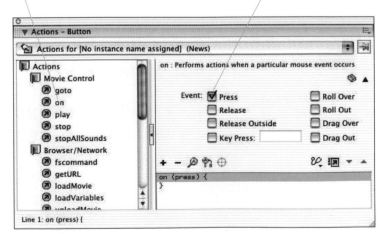

A movie clip can have the same actions added to it as a button.

However, these are triggered by OnClipEvents, rather than OnMouseEvents. The OnClipEvents for a movie clip are:

- *Load, when the movie clip is loaded into the movie*

- *Enter frame, when the Timeline reaches the frame in which the movie clip is placed*

- *Unload, which occurs when the movie clip has finished playing*

- *Mouse down, when the mouse is pressed*

- *Mouse up, when the mouse is released*

- *Mouse move, when the mouse is moved over the movie clip*

- *Key down, when a specific key is pressed*

- *Key up, when a specific key is released*

- *Data, when specific information is entered*

The possible mouse event options for buttons are:

- *Press*, which occurs when the mouse button is pressed while the cursor is within the Hit area of a button

- *Release*, which occurs when the mouse button is released within the Hit area

- *Release Outside*, which occurs when the mouse button is released when the cursor has been dragged outside the Hit area

- *Roll Over*, which occurs when the mouse cursor moves into the Hit area

- *Roll Out*, which occurs when the mouse cursor is moved out of the Hit area

- *Drag Over*, which occurs when the mouse button is held down and dragged out of the Hit area and then back into it

- *Drag Out*, which occurs when the mouse button is clicked within the Hit area and then dragged outside it

- *Key Press*, which can be used to specify a key on the keyboard to trigger the action

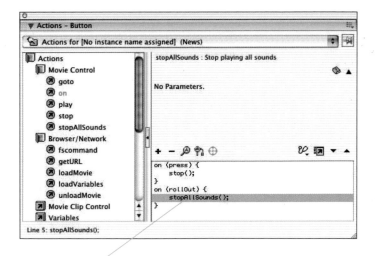

4 Select the actions that will be triggered by the mouse event

Adding movie clips and sounds

Movie clips

To make buttons more versatile it is possible to add movie clips to them. This means that when the button is pressed (or whatever mouse event that has been assigned to it) a movie clip plays. Movie clips can be inserted in the separate states of a button and different ones can be used within the same button. To add a movie clip to a button:

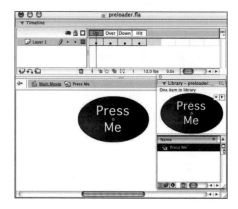

1 Double-click on a button symbol in the Library to access Symbol Editing Mode

If you are using only movie clips to create a button, make sure that the Hit area of the button is big enough to cover the area of the largest movie clip.

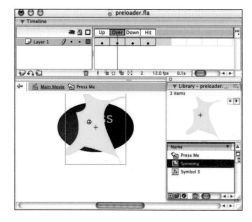

2 Select a state of the button (Up, Over or Down) and drag a movie clip over the button centrepoint. The clip will play when this state of the button is activated

Sounds

Sound files can be added to buttons in the same way as movie clips: open the button in Symbol Editing Mode, select the Up, Over or Down state and drag a sound file from the Library onto the Stage. This is a useful technique to alert the user to whether they have performed a particular action with the button i.e. one sound for when they press the button and another for when they release it. Different sounds can be added to the first three states of a button.

Creating disjoint rollovers

When a basic button is created it is often in the form of a simple rollover i.e. when the cursor moves over the button it changes in appearance. This is an effective technique for buttons on websites, as a subtle change of colour or text can have a significant impact on the user. However, buttons are a lot more versatile than this and they can also be used to create disjoint rollovers. This is when the rollover (Over) portion of the button appears in a different place to the button itself. To create a disjoint rollover:

1 Create a new button and enter content for the Up state

It is best to keep the content for the Down state the same as for the Over state. Otherwise the effect can become overdone, with too much happening at once.

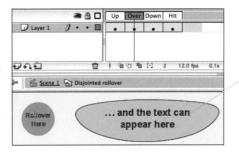

2 Enter content for the Over state, some at a different point to the Up state

When adding the Hit area for a disjoint rollover button, make sure that it only covers the same area as the content in the Up state, not the Over or Down states. Otherwise, the effect will be activated at the wrong time i.e. when you rollover the area of the Over state rather than just the Up state.

3 Enter content for the Down and Hit states. For the Down state this can be the same as the Over state or different. When the button is activated it appears like this:

4 When the button is rolled over, the content for the Over state appears. This is the disjoint effect

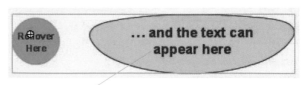

Adding invisible buttons

On some occasions it is useful to have invisible buttons in a Flash movie. These are buttons that have no visible content in either the Up, Over or Down state, but they do have a hit area. Button actions can then be added to the button so that the user can interact with the movie without knowing it. One use for invisible buttons is in the creation of rollover navigation bars (see the next page). To create an invisible button:

1 Create a new symbol and give it a Button behavior and a recognisable name

Invisible buttons can be placed behind text, to give the user the impression that the action is connected with the text block when in fact it is part of the button.

2 Insert a keyframe into the Up state of the button, but do not put any content on the Stage. Repeat this for the Over and Down states but enter content for the Hit state

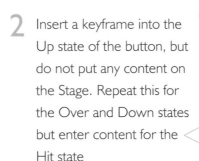

When an instance of an invisible button is created on the Stage, the Hit area is visible, so that you know the exact location of the button.

The Button Actions panel is accessed by clicking once on the button instance on the Stage and selecting Window>Actions from the Menu bar.

3 Drag an instance of the invisible button onto the Stage. Access the Actions panel and add any required actions to the button

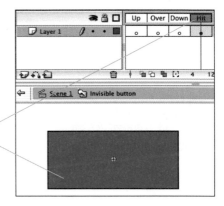

Creating rollover navigation bars

Rollover navigation bars are an increasingly popular way for Web designers to provide a means of navigation around sites. They are a set of buttons that, when a mouse event occurs, reveal submenus for that particular topic. The user can then click on the submenu, or, if they roll away from the submenu button, they are taken back to the start of the menu. This is achieved with a mixture of visible and invisible buttons and the corresponding button actions. These can be written in JavaScript, but it also possible to create them in Flash (for which no programming knowledge is required):

Before you start creating a rollover navigation bar, sketch it out on a piece of paper first. This way you will have a clear understanding of what is required in each frame.

1 Create a button symbol and place an instance of it on the Stage in frame 1 of the movie

The reason for putting a Stop action in frame 1 is to ensure that this frame remains visible when the movie is opened, rather than it starting to play through the rest of the frames.

2 Access the Frame Actions panel and enter a Stop action by double-clicking it

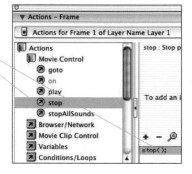

Be careful if you are using a Flash rollover navigation bar when using a website that contains frames and framesets. This is because it can cause real confusion when targeting the links in the navigation bar.

3 Select the button instance by clicking it once and access the Button Actions panel. Select Release for the OnMouseEvent and then select the Go To and Stop action. Enter Frame 2 as the target frame for the action

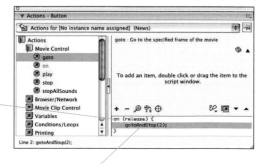

4 Insert a keyframe in frame 2 and insert the content for the submenu. This can consist of drawing objects and text. They do not need to be created as buttons because all of the functionality will be added with

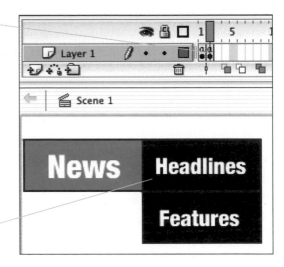

A Stop action ensures that the movie is halted at the specified frame. It remains like this until another action is activated i.e. a Play action or a Go To action.

invisible buttons. Add a stop action into the frame that contains this content. This will ensure that the movie stops at this point and so allows the menu to be displayed

5 Create an invisible button, which is exactly the same size as the area for each submenu. Place an invisible button over each submenu area, so that it covers it completely

The invisible buttons could be placed on a layer above the submenus. However, since there are no other object actions on this layer, there is nothing that could conflict with the action in the invisible buttons.

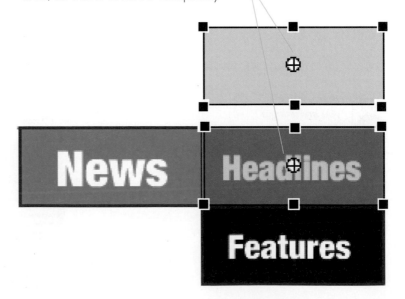

In the example on the right the invisible button will keep the user on the existing frame, i.e. the submenus, when they rollover the invisible button. If they roll away from it, in any direction, they will be taken to frame 1. However, if they press and release the button, the Get URL action will be activated.

Using this technique, complex rollover navigation bars can be created. Add more buttons to the main menu in frame 1 and then create the submenus for each item in subsequent frames, i.e. 2, 3, 4 etc. Add the appropriate actions to all of the buttons in the main menu, so that they go to the correct frame for the corresponding submenu.

In all of the subsequent frames, add Stop actions and also the invisible button that takes the movie back to the main menu (i.e. frame 1) if one of the submenu options is not selected.

Select View>Rulers from the Menu bar to get a better idea of the dimensions of the navigation bar.

6 Give each instance of the invisible button the same set of Object Actions:

- OnMouseEvent: Rollover
- Go To and Stop, frame 2;
- OnMouseEvent: Rollout
- Go To and Stop, frame 1:
- OnMouseEvent: Release
- Get URL, (enter required URL)

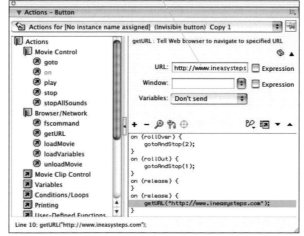

7 When the rollover navigation bar is completed, select Modify> Document and enter dimensions for

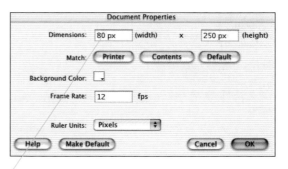

the width and height of the movie to match the size of the navigation bar. This way, when the movie is inserted into a Web page there will be no wasted space around it.

ActionScript

Using Expert Mode

If you are not experienced in using ActionScript then creating actions in Normal Mode, as shown on the previous pages, will probably suit your purposes more than adequately. However, if you do know some ActionScript then you may find this a useful option. Also, if you can program in JavaScript then you will find this familiar because in Flash MX the two languages now share the same programming syntax.

Expert Mode allows you to write your own ActionScript code or edit existing code. You can add actions from the Toolkit on the left of the actions panel, but there are no Basic actions available (it is presumed that if you know some ActionScript, then you will be able to create the coding for these yourself). Also, there are no parameters available for actions in Expert Mode – these too have to be entered manually. To access Expert Mode:

Preferences can be set for the appearance of ActionScript code. To do this, select Edit>Preferences (Windows) or Flash> Preferences (Mac) from the Menu bar and then click on the ActionScript Editor tab. The preferences can then be set in this dialog box.

You can return to Normal Mode from Expert Mode by clicking on the View Options button in Expert Mode and selecting Normal Mode from the menu.

1 In either the Button or Frame Actions panel, click on the View Options button and select Expert Mode

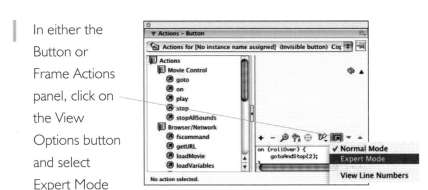

2 The available action groups are displayed here

3 ActionScript can be entered or edited here

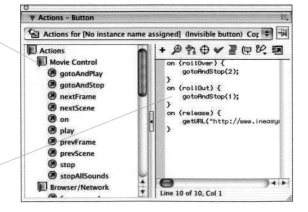

Using ActionScript

ActionScript is an object-orientated computer programming language that shares considerable similarities with JavaScript, including the coding syntax. It is used to add the elements of interactivity into a Flash movie and, if used to its full potential, it is an extremely powerful tool. However, this also means that it is not something that can be picked up in a few days. If you have experience of other programming languages then it will be easier to get to grips with ActionScript, but if you want to learn it from scratch, it will probably take several months to become proficient. ActionScript is created in the Actions panel which can be accessed by selecting Window>Actions from the Menu bar. Within the Actions panel there are a number of options for enhancing the process of creating ActionScript:

The ActionScript Dictionary describes the syntax and use of ActionScript elements within Flash MX. This is an invaluable resource if you are going to be creating your own ActionScripts. It can be accessed by selecting Help>ActionScript Dictionary from the Menu bar.

Add a new element to a script

Add a target path for an element

Show code hints

Get a description for a selected item

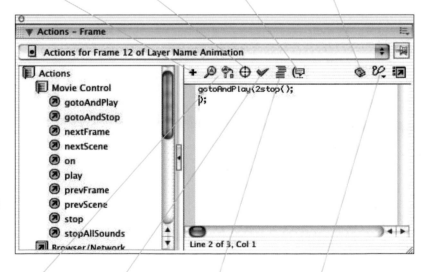

When you insert actions with either the Frame Actions or the Button Actions panels it is worth having a look at the ActionScript code that is created, so that you can become familiar with its appearance.

Find and replace items

Check the syntax

Auto format the code

Debug the code

UI Components

User Interface (UI) Components are a collection of movie clips that can be added to a movie to give it increased interactivity. The UI Components have their parameters created in ActionScript and they are complex movie clips that can be used in items such as online forms or questionnaires for gathering information from users. The reason that they are created with ActionScript is that this is required to analyse the data when it comes back from the movie. To add UI Components:

It is relatively straightforward to add the elements of UI Components onto the Stage. However, it is a lot more complicated to add the interactive element so that they can communicate with a server that is hosting the movie. This requires a good knowledge of computer programming in general and ActionScript in particular.

1 Select Window> Components to view the available pre-defined components

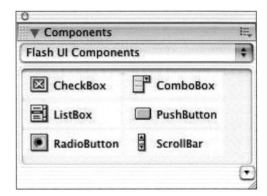

2 To add a component, drag it onto the Stage

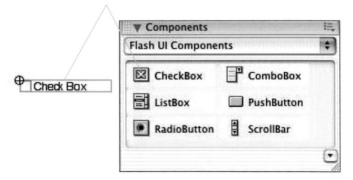

3 Select a component to view its parameters in the Component Properties Inspector

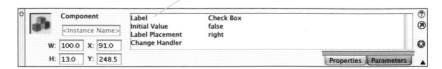

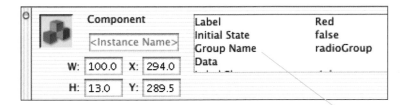

Component		Label	Red
	<Instance Name>	Initial State	false
		Group Name	radioGroup
W: 100.0	X: 294.0	Data	
H: 13.0	Y: 289.5		

4   In the Component Properties Inspector, enter new parameters for the component, such as a new name (Label), whether it is initially checked on or off (Initial State) and the Group Name. This is used for RadioButtons where only one selection can be made from a group of options. In this instance all of the RadioButtons have to have the same Group Name

5   Through the use of UI Components, items such as feedback forms and questionnaires can be created

Some UI Components, such as CheckBoxes, allow for multiple items to be selected. Others, such as RadioButtons, only allow for one choice to be made from the available list.

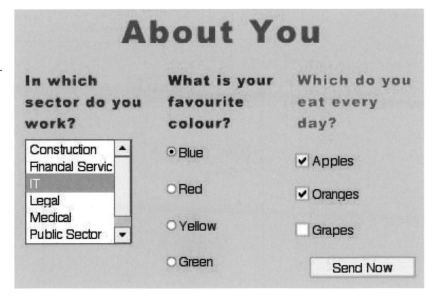

Named anchors

A common feature of Web browsers is the ability to use the Back and Forward buttons to move through previously viewed pages. In Flash MX there is a function for creating movies that can be navigated in the same way in a browser. This is known as named anchors and they can be added to movies to give them this navigational functionality in browsers. To add named anchors:

Select File>Publish Settings from the Menu bar. Click on the HTML tab and select Flash with Named Anchors in the Template box

Named anchors work most effectively if there are no spaces in the name of the anchor. This is because some browsers have problems with filenames, or anchor names, that contain spaces.

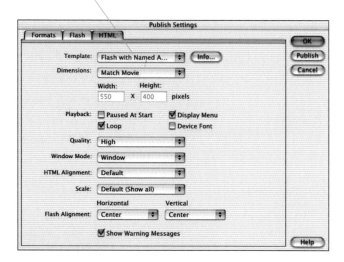

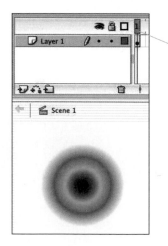

2 Enter content in frame one. Give the frame a name in the Frame Properties Inspector and check on the Named Anchor box

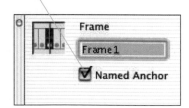

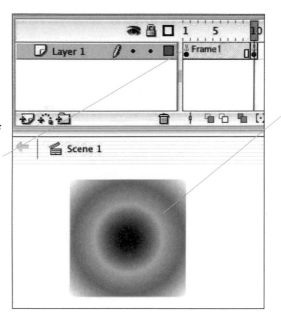

Named anchors are denoted by orange anchors inserted in the Timeline.

3 Add another keyframe and add content on the Stage. Add a named anchor to the frame in the same way as in Step 2 on the facing page

4 When the movie is published and viewed in a browser, navigate through the movie once it has begun playing by using the Forward and Back buttons

If you are using named anchors in a Flash movie, it may be worth entering a note to this effect at the start of the movie. This will alert the user to the fact that they can navigate around the movie using the Back and Forward buttons on the browser. Otherwise, they may not realise that this function is available.

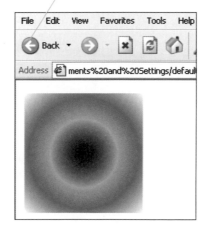

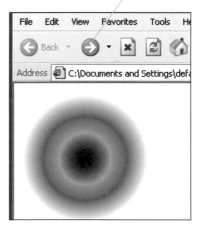

Movie Explorer

When a movie is being created, it is easy to lose track of all of the elements that have been added. In addition to drawing objects, texts and instances, there are also all of the actions and it can be confusing remembering where all of these are and what they do. To simplify matters in this respect, Flash has the Movie Explorer. This displays a graphical and hierarchical layout of all the elements within the movie.

To use the Movie Explorer:

As well as providing a graphical and hierarchical display of the contents of a movie, the Movie Explorer can also perform a number of editing and organisational tasks. This is done through the Options menu, which can be accessed by clicking on the arrow in the top right corner of the Movie Explorer panel.

1 Select Window>Movie Explorer from the Menu bar

2 Click here to display text, symbols, actions, multimedia

3 Click here to display frames and layers, and display settings

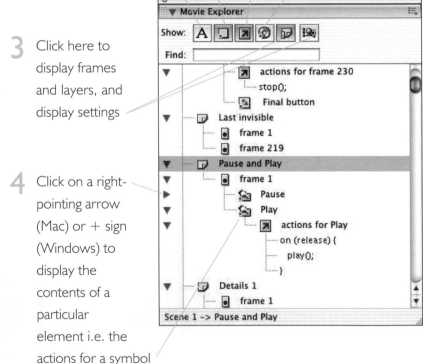

4 Click on a right-pointing arrow (Mac) or + sign (Windows) to display the contents of a particular element i.e. the actions for a symbol

Testing and publishing

The final part of producing a Flash movie is testing it to ensure it works properly and then publishing it for people to see. This chapter looks at ways to test the elements of a movie, set publishing options and then publish a movie, either on the Web or as a stand-alone application.

Covers

Testing options | 172

Testing environment | 174

Preparing to publish | 178

More publishing options | 182

Creating a transparent movie | 183

Publishing a movie | 185

Publishing on the Web | 186

Chapter Eleven

Testing options

As with any project that is going to be viewed by a large audience, it is important to test movies thoroughly before they are published. Within a Flash movie there can be a number of complex elements and it is essential to make sure that everything is working properly, both independently and as part of the whole movie. Flash has several testing options and the ones in the authoring environment are:

The Controller

The Controller is a quick way to test animations without having to leave the authoring environment. Another way is to drag the Playhead along the Timeline, although this may not play it at a consistent speed.

This plays a movie through in the authoring environment. It shows animations but buttons and frame actions are inactive. To use the Controller:

1 Select Window>Toolbars>Controller from the Menu bar (Windows) or Window>Controller (Mac)

2 Use the controls to play the movie

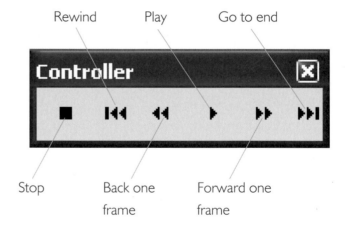

Enable buttons and frames

The Enable Frame Actions and Enable Buttons options should only be used when you want to test these items. Otherwise they could interfere with other editing processes.

Frame actions and buttons can be viewed in the authoring environment:

1 Select Control>Enable Simple Frame Actions (or Control>Enable Simple Buttons) in the Menu bar

When it is first accessed, the testing environment will look similar to the authoring one. The only difference is that most of the Menu bar and toolbar options are greyed out. However, there are a number of features that can be accessed in the testing environment that allow greater versatility when testing a movie. These are looked at on the following pages.

Rather than just testing individual parts of a movie, as with the options in the authoring environment on the facing page, it is also possible to test an entire scene or movie to see how it will appear when it is published.

Testing scenes

To test an individual scene:

1 Open the scene you want to test and select Control>Test Scene from the Menu bar

2 This will open the selected scene and play it in the testing environment. Animations, frame actions and buttons will all be active

Overtime Form

Please complete this form for all overtime worked

Name

Section

Employee Number

Begin by entering your name, as it appears on your payslip. When this step has been completed, click on this button.

Testing movies

HOT TIP

To return to the authoring environment from the testing one, close down the testing window or select File>Close from the Menu bar.

This performs a very similar task to Test Scene, except that it tests all of the scenes in a movie, in the order in which they will play when the movie is published. To test a movie:

1 Select Control>Test Movie from the Menu bar

Control	Window	Help	
Play			Enter
Rewind			Ctrl+Alt+R
Go To End			
Step Forward			.
Step Backward			,
Test Movie			Ctrl+Enter

Testing environment

When a Flash movie is played over a browser on the Web it is impossible to predict how it will appear on every user's computer. This is because of the wide range of browsers being used, processor speeds and modem speeds: on one computer the movie may play perfectly, but on another it may take longer to download and play erratically. Flash has a number of functions to test how a movie will play in different circumstances.

Test movies at the lowest download speed first (14.4K). If they work well at this speed then there should be no problem at the higher speeds. However, test them at the higher ones too, just to make sure.

Testing download speeds

Due to the diversity of modems used by people when accessing the Internet it is certain that your movie will be downloaded at a variety of speeds. You can test how various options will look by using the streaming option in the testing environment:

1 In the testing environment for a scene or a movie, select Debug from the Menu bar and select the required download speed

The User Settings and the Customize option for download speeds can be used for high speed connections or if the movie is being used on an intranet. If this is the case, check the required setting with your system administrator.

2 Select View>Show Streaming to see how your movie will play at the selected download speed

Bandwidth Profiler

A Bandwidth Profiler is available in the testing environment and this can display several items of useful information about the streaming of the movie and how individual frames affect this. To view the Bandwidth Profiler:

Streaming is a technique which allows a movie to start playing when only part of the whole movie has been downloaded. If this works properly the movie should play smoothly throughout.

However, problems can occur if there are very large frames in a movie since the movie will already be playing and the downloading will be slowed down. If the playback of the movie catches up with the streaming download then there could be a pause in the playing of the movie.

1   In the testing environment select View>Bandwidth Profiler from the Menu bar

2   The Bandwidth Profiler is displayed above the movie

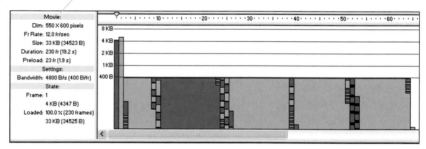

The elements of the Bandwidth Profiler are:

•   *Dim.* This is the dimensions of your movie, in pixels

•   *Fr Rate.* This is the Frames Per Second speed at which your movie is set to play

•   *Size.* This is the file size of the entire movie or scene

•   *Duration.* This is the total number of frames in the movie (or scene). The number beside it, in brackets, is the time the movie (or scene) will take to play, in seconds

- *Preload.* This is the time the movie will take to download before it starts to play. This information is particularly relevant if you want to include a preloader with a movie (see Chapter Ten)

- *Bandwidth.* This is the bandwidth speed that has been selected to test the download speed of the movie

- *Frame.* The first number is where the Playhead is currently situated and the one underneath it displays a selected frame's size in relation to the whole movie

- *Loaded.* The first number displays how many frames of the movie have been downloaded and the one underneath displays the amount of the file that has been downloaded

Streaming Graph

When used in conjunction with the Bandwidth Profiler the Streaming Graph can identify potential problem areas for when a movie is downloading. To access the Streaming Graph:

1 In the testing environment, select View>Streaming Graph

2 Bars above the red line indicate frames that could cause a problem when downloading

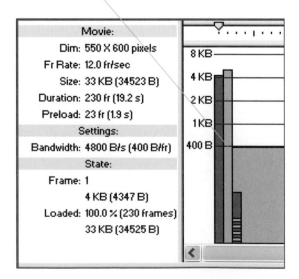

Frame-by-frame graph

Another option for assessing the downloading speed of a movie is the frame-by-frame graph. This shows the size of each frame in a movie. To view the frame-by-frame graph:

1 In the testing environment, select View>Frame By Frame Graph

View	Control	Debug	Window	Help

Zoom In   Ctrl+=
Zoom Out   Ctrl+-
Magnification   ▶

✔ Bandwidth Profiler   Ctrl+B

Show Streaming   Ctrl+Enter
Streaming Graph   Ctrl+G
✔ Frame By Frame Graph   Ctrl+F

2 The size of each individual frame in the movie is displayed in the graph. Select an individual frame to view its properties in the Bandwidth Profiler

If a few frames stand out as being a lot bigger in size than the others in the movie, return to the authoring environment and see if they can be edited.

In the testing environment, select Quality on the View menu and click on either Low, Medium or High to see the movie at a higher or lower quality.

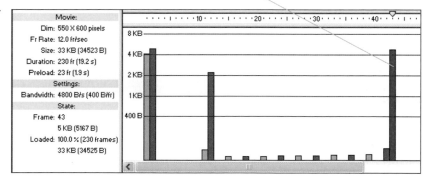

Movie:
Dim: 550 X 600 pixels
Fr Rate: 12.0 fr/sec
Size: 33 KB (34523 B)
Duration: 230 fr (19.2 s)
Preload: 23 fr (1.9 s)
Settings:
Bandwidth: 4800 B/s (400 B/fr)
State:
Frame: 43
5 KB (5167 B)
Loaded: 100.0 % (230 frames)
33 KB (34525 B)

Preparing to publish

The object of creating any Flash movie is to have it published. This can be onto a CD-ROM as a stand-alone application, but the most common use for Flash movies is to publish them on the Web or an intranet.

The method for publishing Flash movies on the Web is to insert them into a HTML document. If you look at the code for a file on the Web containing a Flash movie you may want to run screaming from your computer, never to think of Flash or HTML again. At first sight it does look confusing, even if you have some experience of producing Web pages. The good news is that you only have to specify a few settings and Flash does all of the complicated work for you. This is done by instructing Flash to create a HTML document with the Flash movie inserted in it. However, before this, certain settings can be chosen to determine the way the movie will look when it is published.

Publish settings for the Web

To determine the settings for a movie on the Web:

1   In the authoring environment, select File>Publish Settings

2   Select Flash and HTML as the type. This will create a Flash movie file (Shockwave Flash or .SWF) and a HTML file (.HTM)

If you select HTML as a format for publishing your movie, the Flash option is selected automatically.

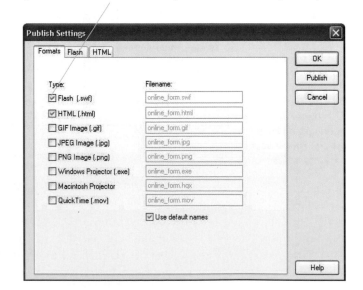

3 In the Publish Settings dialog box select the HTML tab

 Click the Info button next to the Template box for a description of the template and any HTML tags it uses.

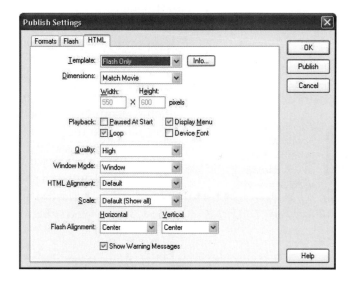

HTML settings

Within the HTML dialog box there are various settings to determine the appearance of the Flash movie in your HTML document:

- *Template*. This is how the movie is inserted into the HTML document. The simplest one is the default, Flash Only, which uses EMBED and OBJECT tags to display the movie depending on which browser it is being viewed on (EMBED for Netscape Navigator or Communicator and OBJECT for Internet Explorer). Some other available templates are: Flash for Pocket PC; Flash with FS Command; Flash with Named Anchor; and Image Map. These can be used to give extra functionality to a movie, but if you are not confident with these then the default is more than adequate

 The options for specifying the dimensions of a published movie do not affect its positioning within the HTML window, just its location in the movie window.

- *Dimensions*. This dictates how the movie will appear within a movie window within the HTML document window. The default is to match the size set in the Movie Properties dialog box. However, the size can also be set in pixels or as a percentage to make the movie larger or smaller than the movie window, as appropriate

- *Playback.* The options here determine the properties for when the movie is played in a browser. These are: Paused At Start, which means the movie does not start playing until the user performs an action such as clicking a button; Display Menu, which displays a contextual menu about the Flash Player if the user right-clicks (Windows) or Ctrl+clicks (Mac); Loop, which will cause the movie to keep playing after its initial playback; and Device Font (Windows only), which substitutes suitable fonts if the ones in the movie are not installed on the user's computer

There is also an option for Window Mode which can be used to create movies with transparent backgrounds (see page 183).

- *Quality.* This can be used to get the best balance between playback speed and image quality. The options range from Low, which is the fastest speed and the lowest image quality, to Best, which offers the top image quality but the slowest playback speed

- *HTML Alignment.* This can be used if you create a HTML page with other items in addition to the Flash movie. This allows you to align the movie with the other items on the page. The options are Left, Right, Top and Bottom

In order to get the correct position for your published movie, experiment with the Dimensions, Scale and Flash Alignment settings to see how different combinations appear in a browser.

- *Scale.* If you have changed the dimensions of the movie from its original settings this can be used to determine how it is scaled within the movie window. The options are: Show All, which scales the movie proportionately to fit the movie window; No Border, which will display the movie at its actual size even if it is bigger than the movie window; and Exact Fit, which scales the movie to fit exactly into the whole movie window

- *Flash Alignment.* This can be used to determine the movie's position within the movie window. The options are for Horizontal – Left, Center and Right; and for Vertical – Top, Center and Bottom

HTML editors can be used to include additional content, as well as the Flash movie.

- *Show Warning Messages.* This alerts the user to any problems with the HTML coding

Flash settings

In addition to determining the HTML settings for a movie, the same can be done for Flash settings.

Select the Flash tab in the Publish Settings dialog box

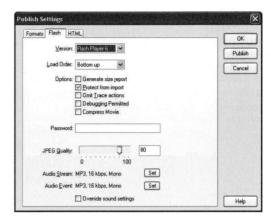

Flash MX movies are capable of playing on any earlier version of the Flash Player, using the Version setting.

The Flash settings are:

- *Version.* This can be used so earlier versions of the Flash Player can view your movie

- *Load Order.* This lets you set the order in which layers within a frame are loaded into the browser

- *Generate size report.* For creating a report on the size of each frame

When setting the JPEG quality, a setting of '0' will create images with the lowest quality and '100' the highest.

- *Protect from import.* This stops anyone copying your movie and using it as their own

- *Omit Trace actions.* This stops anyone being able to look at the code that makes up a movie

- *Debugging Permitted.* This can be used with the Password option to allow remote debugging of movies

- *Compress movie.* This makes the file as small as possible

Stream sounds are those that download while the movie is playing; event sounds are those that are played when a specific action occurs, such as a button being pressed.

- *JPEG Quality.* To set the quality of JPEG images

- *Audio Stream.* To compress streamed sounds

- *Audio Event.* To compress event sounds

More publishing options

Although HTML is the most common way to publish Flash movies there are a number of other options, which can all be accessed by selecting the Formats tab in the Publish Settings dialog box. The other formats are:

- *Projectors.* These are stand-alone applications that act like mini programs, that can be played on almost any computer. Everything that is needed to play the movie is contained within the projector file and it is just a case of opening it from a CD-ROM, a floppy disk or a hard drive

- *QuickTime.* This is a video and multimedia file format that has been developed by Apple and it is widely used for playing videos on the Web. The QuickTime format has its own dialog box and a Flash movie can be incorporated with other items in a QuickTime movie. The QuickTime dialog box lets you set the size of the QuickTime movie and how the Flash movie interacts with other elements. Download the QuickTime plug-in from www.apple.com/

- *Graphic formats.* There are dialog boxes for three different graphic formats: GIFs, JPEGs and PNGs. This allows you to apply a variety of settings to determine how these images are displayed in the published movie

All formats for Flash movies (except Projector) have their own dialogs. Click a tab in the Publish Settings dialog to access them

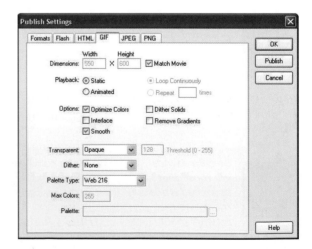

Creating a transparent movie

One of the most effective, and frequently overlooked, uses for Flash is the creation of small movies that can be included as part of a HTML page on the Web, without dominating the rest of the content. This can be particularly useful for company logos and the suchlike. With items like this, it is useful to be able to make the background of the movie transparent, so that when it is placed on a Web page, the background of the HTML page is visible behind the Flash movie. To achieve this:

The default setting for the rulers is pixels. If you want to change this, select Modify>Document from the Menu bar and select the required unit of measurement from the Ruler>Units box.

1 Create a Flash movie that contains a logo or similar icon. Make sure the rulers are showing by selecting View>Rulers

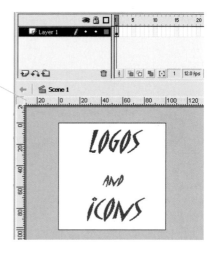

If you do not modify the size of the movie to match the content on the Stage, the transparent effect will still be applied to the whole movie. However, you will have less scope for adding content around it on the HTML page because the movie will take up a greater amount of space and you will not be able to place any content on top of it.

2 Select Modify>Document from the Menu bar and enter the dimensions of the movie so that the object takes up all of the space on the Stage

3 Select File>Publish Settings from the Menu bar. Select the HTML tab and in the Window Mode box select Transparent Windowless

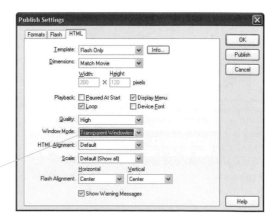

For more information on Dreamweaver, see Computer Step's 'Dreamweaver MX in easy steps' title.

4 Publish the movie (see the facing page) so that a HTML file is created. Open this in a Web authoring program such as Dreamweaver

5 Enter a background for the HTML page. The Flash movie icon will appear on top of it

When creating the HTML page for the transparent Flash movie, use the one that was produced during the Publish operation in Flash itself, and then add additional content to it. The command to make the movie transparent is inserted into the HTML document when it is created in Flash.

6 Save the HTML page and view it in a browser. The background colour will be visible through the Flash movie. If it were transparent, it would look like the illustration on the right

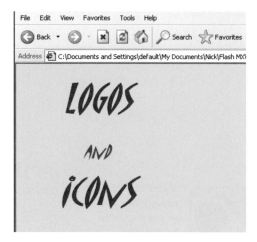

Flash movies like this can be resized within a Web authoring program in the same way as you would resize a graphical image. Since they are created with vectors they do not lose any definition.

7 If the background were not transparent, it would look like this

Publishing a movie

Once you have chosen the format(s) for your movie and assigned the necessary settings, it is time to publish your work.

Previewing

Before the movie is actually published it is possible to see exactly what it will look like in each of the chosen formats:

Select File>Publish Preview from the Menu bar and select the format in which you want to view the movie

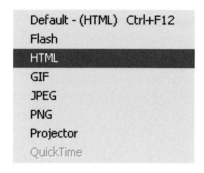

It is possible to publish a movie into several different formats. Select each format in the Publish Settings dialog. When you select Publish, Flash will create the appropriate files for all of these formats.

Publishing

If you are satisfied with the preview of your movie you can then publish it:

Select File>Publish from the Menu bar. The following files are created

After step 1, Flash creates files for all of the formats that were selected in the Publish Settings dialog and places them in the same folder as the original movie.

Authoring file (.FLA)   HTML file

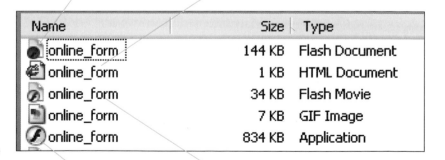

The Projector format creates the largest file size of all Flash formats.

Projector file   Movie file (.SWF)

Publishing on the Web

If you are publishing a Flash movie on the Web you will need to upload your HTML file and the Flash movie file (.SWF) to the Web server where your site will be hosted. Check with your Internet Service Provider (ISP), or system administrator if you are publishing over an intranet, that they are capable of displaying Flash and ask if there are any specific settings they require.

Once your HTML page is published the source code will look something like this:

A HTML file is made up of a set of instructions that tell the browser what to display at certain points. Since the Flash movie is referred to in the HTML document it has to be on the server too so that the browser can display it.

Flash generates the HTML coding during the Publish process

Of the two files that are created when a movie is put together, the movie itself has a .SWF extension and the authoring file has a .FLA extension.

(The .SWF file is the one that is uploaded to the Web server, along with the HTML file.)

Using a HTML editor

Flash movies can make up the entire contents of a HTML document. However, if you use a HTML editor (such as Macromedia Dreamweaver, Adobe GoLive or Microsoft FrontPage), it is possible to create additional content on the HTML page. This is an excellent way to combine a Flash movie into a larger HTML document on the Web. There are two important considerations when you are publishing Flash sites on the Web:

- Always include a plain HTML version of your site, for users who do not have the Flash Player installed, or who do not want to download it

- Include a link for those users who want to download the latest version of the Flash Player

Index

A

Accessibility   27–28
Actions
    Button   144
    Deleting   147
    Frame   144
        Adding   145
    Go To
        Adding   149–150
    OnClipEvent   157
    OnMouseEvent   156
    Stop   128
    Stop and Play
        Adding   148
    Types   146–147
ActionScript   10, 146
    Expert Mode   164
    Using   165
Adobe
    GoLive   186
    Illustrator   90
    Photoshop   92
AIFF files   95
Anchors. *See* Named anchors
Animation
    Animating text   138
    Basics   120
    Frame-by-frame   11, 120
        Creating   126–128
    Guided   11
    Motion guides   132–133
        Orientation   134
    Motion tweens   120
        Creating   129–130
        Editing   131
    Shape tweens   120
        Creating   135–136
        Shape hints   137
Anti-aliasing   146
Apple   182
Arrow tool
    Selecting with   48–49

B

Backgrounds
    Creating with frames   104
Bandwidth   8, 175–176
    Profiler   175
        Dim   175
        Duration   175
        Fr Rate   175
        Frame   176
        Loaded   176
        Preload   176
        Size   175
Bitmaps   9, 81, 89–90
    As fills   93–94
    As symbols   77
    Converting items into   90
    Importing   70, 91
    Properties   92
    Types   90
BMPs   90
Brush tool   42
Button symbols
    Creating   153–155
Buttons   11, 76–77, 79, 81–82, 84–85
    Actions   11
    Adding actions to   156–157
    Adding movie clips to   158, 160
    Adding sound to   158, 160
    Invisible
        Adding   160

C

Circles
    Drawing   38
Color palette   61–63, 65, 67

Colours
  Gradient fills
    Adding 65–66
    Editing 68
    Linear 62
    Radial 62
  Selecting 70
  Solid 62
    Creating 63–64
  Swapping 69
Compression 9
Controller 172
Corner points 48
  Adding 55
Curve points 48, 54
Cut-aways. *See* Objects: Creating cut-aways

D

Digital cameras 90–91
Disjoint rollovers. *See* Rollovers: Disjoint: Creating
Distorting. *See* Free Transform tool: Distorting
Dots Per Inch 92
DPI. *See* Dots Per Inch
Dreamweaver. *See* Macromedia: Dreamweaver
Dropper tool 45

E

E-commerce 10
EMBED tag 179
Envelope. *See* Free Transform tool: Envelope
Eraser tool 46
Expert Mode. *See* ActionScript: Expert Mode

F

File extensions 17
Fill Transform tool 67–68

Fills 32
  Reshaping 55
Fireworks. *See* Macromedia: Fireworks
Flash
  Components 14
  Downloading 12
  Environment 14
  Evolution 8
  Home Page 12
  How it works 9
  Installing 13
  Movies 9–10
  Projectors 10
  Trial version 12
  Uses for 10–11
Flash Player 10
  Downloading 12
  Link for downloading 186
Frame rate 103
Frame-by-frame animation. *See* Animation: Frame-by-frame
Frame-by-frame graphs 177
Frames 16–18, 21–22, 24, 102
  Comments 108
  Copying 107
  Creating backgrounds with 104
  Deleting 107
  Keyframes. *See* Keyframes
  Labels 108
  Moving 107
  Properties 108
  Regular 104
    Adding 105
  Sequences 104
    Defined 103
  Setting movie length with 104
Free Transform tool
  Distorting 53
  Envelope 53
  Resizing 52
  Rotating and skewing 52
Freehand. *See* Macromedia: Freehand
FrontPage. *See* Microsoft: FrontPage

G

GIFs 9, 90, 182
GoLive. *See* Adobe: GoLive
Gradients. *See* Colours: Gradient fills
Graphical Interchange Format. *See* GIFs

Graphics. *See* Symbols: Graphics
Grid   127

H

Hexadecimal values   64
HTML   10–11, 178, 181–186
   Settings   179–180

I

Illustrator. *See* Adobe: Illustrator
Ink Bottle tool   43
Instances   77–78, 83, 87
   Defined   76
   Editing   88
Interactivity   11
   Types   144
Internet   174
   Explorer   179
   Publishing to   186
Internet Service Providers. *See* ISPs
Invisible buttons. *See* Buttons: Invisible
ISPs   186

J

JavaScript   146, 161, 164–165
Joint Photographic Experts Group. *See* JPEGs
JPEGs   9, 90, 92, 181–182

K

Kerning   71
Keyframes   102–105, 107, 111, 120–122, 126–130, 132, 135, 138, 145, 152, 155, 160, 162, 169
   Adding   106
   Blank   154

L

Lasso tool   70, 93
   Selecting with   50
Layers   97, 119–121, 123–124, 126, 132–134, 136, 138–140, 144, 151, 162, 170
   Copying   112
   Current mode   113
   Defined   109
   Deleting   112
   Folders   115
   Hidden mode   113
   Inserting   111
   Locked mode   113
   Locking   109
   Mask
      Creating   116–118, 167
   Outline mode   113
   Properties   114
   Renaming   111
   Stacking   109–110
Library   17, 76–78, 91–92, 96
   Accessing   78
   Creating new folders   79
   Deleting items   79
   Menu   80–81
   Opening other libraries   81
Line segments   48
Line tool   35
Lines
   Reshaping a curved line   55
   Reshaping straight lines   54
Looping   150

M

N

Macromedia   12–13
  Dreamweaver   184, 186
  Fireworks   92
  Freehand   90
Magic Wand   70, 93
Mask layers.   *See* Layers: Mask
Menu bar   21
Menus
  Contextual   21
  Control   21
  Edit   21
  File   21
  Help   21
  Insert   21
  Modify   21
  Text   21
  View   21, 24
  Window   21
Microsoft
  FrontPage   11
  PowerPoint   11
Modems   174
Morphing.   *See* Tweening
Motion guides.   *See* Animation: Motion guides
Motion tweens.   *See* Animation: Motion tweens
Mouse events
  Drag Out   157
  Drag Over   157
  Key Press   157
  Press   157
  Release   157
  Release Outside   157
  Roll Out   157
  Roll Over   157
Movie clips.   *See* Symbols: Movie clips
Movie Explorer   170
Movies
  Previewing   185
  Publishing   185
  Testing   174–177
  Transparent
    Creating   183–184
MP3   95
Multimedia   8

Named anchors   143
  Adding   168–169
Navigation bars
  Creating   161–163
Netscape Navigator   179

O

OBJECT tag   179
Objects
  Aligning   56
  Breaking apart   51
  Creating cut-aways   59
  Grouping   51
  Overlay level   30–32
    Selecting   33
  Reshaping   53–55
  Resizing   52
  Stacking   58
  Stage level   30–32
    Selecting   33
OnClipEvents.   *See* Actions: OnClipEvent
Onion skinning   122–123, 128, 130, 136
OnMouseEvents.   *See* Actions: OnMouseEvent
Oval tool   38
Overlay level objects.   *See* Objects: Overlay level

P

Paint Bucket tool   44
Panels   14, 23, 34
  Alignment   56
  Button Actions   156, 160–161, 165
  Character   71
  Frame Actions   145, 147–149, 151–152, 161, 164

Mixer   69
   Creating colours   64
Scene   125
Tools   52–53, 64, 67, 69, 71
   Tools itemised   34
Paragraph properties   73
Paste in Place   60
Pen tool   36
Pencil tool   40–41
PICTs   90
Pixel snapping   57
Playhead   103, 105, 122–123, 126, 130
PNGs   9, 90, 182
Portable Network Group. *See* PNGs
PowerPoint. *See* Microsoft: PowerPoint
Preloaders
   Inserting   151–152
Projectors   182
Properties Inspector   14, 22–23, 27–28, 34–35, 38,
     40, 43–45, 71, 73, 88, 98, 108, 131, 134, 136,
     138, 166–168
Publish settings   178
Publishing   185
   File formats   185
   Flash settings   181
   HTML   180
   Preparations   178–181
   Previewing   185
   Templates   179
   To the Web   186

Q

QuickStart templates   25–26
QuickTime   10, 182

R

Rectangle tool   39
Resizing. *See* Free Transform tool: Resizing
Resolution   92
Rollovers
   Disjoint
     Creating   159

Navigation bars
   Creating   161–163
Rotating and skewing. *See* Free Transform tool: Rotating
   and skewing
Rulers   19

S

Scanners   91
Scenes
   Adding   124–125
   Defined   124
   Renaming   125
   Testing   173
Selecting
   Lines   48
   Objects   48
     Freehand selection   50
     Parts of   49
     Polygon selection   50
Setting movie length   104
Shape hints. *See* Animation: Shape tweens
Shape recognition   41
   Assistance   41
Shape tweens. *See* Animation: Shape tweens
Shift-Select   48
Shockwave Flash   178
Sound   95
   Collections   95
   Creating   95
   Editing   97–98
   Event driven   95
   Importing   96
   Streamed   95
   Volume
     Fading   98
     Increasing   97
Sounds
   As symbols   77
Stage   17
   Colour   18
   Grid   19
   View settings   24
Stage level objects. *See* Objects: Stage level
Stand-alone applications   148
Streaming   8–9, 151, 175
   Graph   176
Strokes   32
Subselect tool   37
Symbol Editing Mode   86, 154

Symbols
  Behaviors 77
  Creating 83–85
  Defined 76–77
  Edit in Place 87
  Editing 87
  Graphics 77
  Movie clips 77, 85, 141

Templates. *See* QuickStart Templates
Testing
  Authoring environment 172
  Download speeds 174
  Options 172–173
  Testing environment 172
Text
  Adding 71–72
  Alignment 73
  Animating 138
  Box 72
  Formatting 73
  Label 72
  Paragraph formatting 73
  Reshaping 74
  Resizing 74
  Rotating 74
Text tool 34, 71–74
Timeline 16, 26, 103, 121
Toolbars 20
Tweening 11, 102, 119–120, 129, 135–137, 140, 142

UI Components 166–167
Undo command 112
URLs 146, 163
User Interface. *See* UI Components

Vector-based graphics 9, 34
Video
  Adding 99
  Manipulating 100

Web authoring 10
Web Safe palette 63–64
Work Area 17, 24, 126
World Wide Web 8

Zip drives 91